Eric Foner is a Pulitzer Prize-winning historian and DeWitt Clinton Professor of History at Columbia University. He is one of America's leading historians of the American Civil War and Reconstruction Era. His books include *Free Soil, Free Labor, Free Men: The Ideology of the Republican Party Before the Civil War* (1969); *Reconstruction: America's Unfinished Revolution, 1863–1877* (1988); and *The Fiery Trial: Abraham Lincoln and American Slavery* (2010).

"Nothing could be more timely, more needed than this collection of Eric Foner's work. For the depth and breadth of his intellect as well as the clarity and precision of his language, he has peers but no superiors. Throughout his career, Professor Foner has enlightened and provoked us to become our better selves."

Toni Morrison,
Winner of the Nobel Prize in Literature

"An extraordinary collection of essays, at once erudite and unflinching, from one of America's most gifted historians."

Jill Lepore,
David Woods Kemper '41 Professor of
American History at Harvard University

"Over a span of almost four decades, Eric Foner has consistently illuminated the conflicts of the present with an acute understanding of and sensibility for the past. Henry Ford thought history was 'more or less bunk.' Read *Battles for Freedom* and learn why it is indispensable to being a good citizen."

Michael Kazin,
editor of *Dissent* and author of *War Against War:*
The American Fight for Peace, 1914–1918

BATTLES
FOR
FREEDOM

THE USE AND ABUSE OF AMERICAN HISTORY

ERIC FONER

I.B. TAURIS
LONDON · NEW YORK

The Nation.

Published in 2017 by
I.B.Tauris & Co. Ltd and The Nation Company, LLC
London • New York
www.ibtauris.com

ISBN: 978 1 78453 769 2
eISBN: 978 1 78672 144 0
ePDF: 978 1 78673 144 9

A full CIP record for this book is available from the British Library
A full CIP record is available from the Library of Congress

Library of Congress Catalog Card Number: available

Printed and bound by CPI Group (UK) Ltd, Croydon, CR0 4YY

Contents

Introduction

BY RANDALL KENNEDY

MICHAEL R. KLEIN PROFESSOR, HARVARD LAW SCHOOL

For nearly four decades, *The Nation* has been the main forum in which Eric Foner has brought his encyclopedic knowledge of American history to bear on discussions of current affairs. He has done so with remarkable verve, care and insight. He is a model intellectual.

The writings collected here cover a wide range of subjects, two of which, often overlapping, are particularly salient: the politics of history and the politics of race. In dispatches from the culture wars, Foner offers shrewd reports on various controversies and their recurring casts of characters: authorities who try to impose a relentlessly celebratory depiction of the American past, revisionists who insist upon more realistic portrayals, and the scourges of "political correctness," a motley coalition he describes as "longtime conservatives, onetime radicals and academics enamored of campus life before the advent of large numbers of women and minority students."

Characteristic of Foner's contributions to these debates is "Fighting for the West," a piece written with historian Jon Wiener, in which the authors describe a fight that erupted over an exhibit at the Smithsonian Institution's National Museum of American Art, "The West as America: Reinterpreting Images of the Frontier, 1820-1920." The exhibit featured iconic imagery by esteemed artists such as Frederic Remington, but it also questioned that iconography in commentaries that elicited considerable ire. Charles Krauthammer complained that the commentaries displayed "a crude half-baked Marxist meanness" that expressed "contempt for every achievement of Western expansion." A reviewer for the *Washington Post* called the show "the most cynical exhibit … ever presented under the aegis of your tax dollars and mine," asserting that it "trashe[d] … most of our national history." The famously cantankerous Republican senator from Alaska, Ted Stevens, held a congressional hearing in which he accused the museum of advancing a leftist agenda and threatened to pare its budget.

Foner and Wiener champion the exhibit, praising the curators for suggesting that viewers bring a questioning attitude toward the artwork displayed—that they ask, among other things, whether the artist was engaged simply in straightforward documentation or in rendering an idealized or derogatory depiction that says as much about the artist and his assumptions as about his purported subject. The piece lauds the curators for informing audiences about prejudices that should be considered in interpreting artistic portrayals of the "winning" of the West, noting, for example, that in evaluating Remington's portrayals of cowboys and Indians it is useful to keep in mind his detestation of Native Americans and others he deemed to be despicable inferiors.

"Jews—inguns—chinamen—Italians—Huns," Remington wrote, were "the rubish of the earth I hate."

Foner and Wiener commend the museum for including not only familiar tales about white pioneers, but also unfamiliar information about the mistreatment of Indian nations and environmental degradation. "Long devoted simply to collecting and displaying memorabilia of prominent men and emblems of American greatness," the Smithsonian and other museums, they observe, "are now seeking to present a more complex, diversified and critical portrait of the American past." Properly conveyed, the story of westward expansion "is a story of success and failure, heroism and betrayal, capitalist triumph and labor exploitation. Colorado miners and Mexican peons are as much a part of the story as pioneers on the Oregon Trail. In other words, the West's development was a complex history, not a simple heroic progress."

Confronting the "political correctness" canard, Foner concedes that some revisionists have probably gone overboard in their denunciations. He rightly notes, however, that such abuses are a relatively minor problem that is eclipsed by much larger threats to American cultural life, including "dwindling public funds, rising corporate influence, the fragmentation of scholarship and widespread illiteracy." Addressing the charge that left revisionists pose a danger due to alleged efforts at political indoctrination, Foner aptly observes that "it is the right, not the left, that today poses the real threat to intellectual freedom." Left revisionists are not the ones who threaten museums with defunding, prompting their frightened staffs to tone down presentations that might offend thin-skinned observers.

That is the handiwork of right-wing politicians and publicists who indulge in cultural coercions of all sorts, free of worry that they will incur the wrath of the *Wall Street Journal* and other forums of reaction that are somehow blind to repression unless it can be tarred as "left" or "liberal" or "multicultural."

* * *

Throughout his writings, Foner propounds the absolute centrality of freedom of expression to any attractive conception of the good life in America. Civil liberties, he remarks, "are the inheritance of a long history of struggles: by abolitionists for the ability to hold meetings and publish their views in the face of mob violence; by labor leaders for the power to organize unions ... ; by feminists for the right to disseminate birth-control information without being charged with violating the obscenity laws," and so on. His attentiveness to the need for, and vulnerability of, open, robust, uninhibited debate stems, in part, from a sad personal experience. In "The Education of Richard Hofstadter," a magnificent essay about his dissertation adviser, Foner notes poignantly that one of Hofstadter's early jobs became available when Foner's own father was fired in the course of an anti-Communist purge of college teachers in New York in the 1940s.

The struggle for racial justice is Foner's other over-arching subject. He wants everyone to learn about, recognize and acknowledge the depth, pervasiveness and continuing influence of racial oppression. Aware of the many layers of ignorance, denial, prejudice and delusion that hinder an appropriate under-standing of American racial conflict, Foner seeks to break through complacency by deploying terms that anger many Americans. Hence he describes the destruction of Native American nations as "our home-grown holocaust" and slavery as "our home-grown crime against humanity." In a review of *Lies Across America: What Our Historic Sites Get Wrong* by James W. Loewen (a "one-man historical truth squad"), Foner rails against the amnesia, evasions and misrepresentations that remain especially evident in popular history. He disapproves of tours of plantations at which guides focus on furniture, gardens and architecture to the exclusion of any mention or display of whips and chains. He is disgusted by the fact that in Tennessee there are more memorializations of Nathan Bedford Forrest than any other figure in the state's history (including president Andrew Jackson) despite Forrest having been a slave trader, founder of the Ku Klux Klan and the commander of Confederate troops that massacred black Union soldiers after they had surrendered. He notes sarcastically that "only one transgression was sufficiently outrageous to disqualify Confederate leaders from the pantheon of heroes." That "crime" was to support extending rights to blacks after the Civil War, a reason for the virtual invisibility of Confederate generals such as James Longstreet and James Fleming. Foner is appalled that in Louisiana markers celebrate the life of politician Leander Perez for his "dedicated service" but say nothing that would alert today's public that in the 1960s Perez was a rabid white supremacist who called blacks "animals right out of the jungle."

Two particularly instructive pieces here are "Hiring Quotas for White Males Only," a defense of affirmative action, and "The

Great Divide," a defense of integration. To those who allege that affirmative action undercuts the self-confidence of its supposed beneficiaries, Foner responds: "I have yet to meet the white male in whom special favoritism (getting a job, for example, through relatives ... or because of racial discrimination ...) fostered doubt about his own abilities." To those who allege that affirmative action is the great impediment to the triumph of meritocracy, Foner declares: "Let us not delude ourselves ... into thinking that eliminating affirmative action will produce a society in which rewards are based on merit. Despite our rhetoric, equal opportunity has never been the American way. For nearly all our history, affirmative action has been a prerogative of white men."

In the article championing integration, Foner resists the notion that, regardless of their politics, whites are almost inescapably undependable allies in struggles for racial justice. Throughout the history of the United States, Foner declares, "countless whites have fought for a society in which all citizens enjoyed equal rights and equal opportunities." Similarly, he refutes charges that integrationist politics are necessarily naïve, futile, old-hat. "Integration," he asserts, "is a very radical idea, not a stuffy nostrum ... our society can far more easily accommodate a program of separatism ... than a program of genuine integration." What, for him, is "genuine integration"? It is *not* the mere "absorption of blacks into the pre-existing white social order but the *transformation* of American society so as to give real meaning to the principle of equality. Properly understood, integration means not only the removal of economic, social and political obstacles to full participation in every area of American life but changes in the contours of personal life so that friendship, comradeship and intimacy between the races can become far more common than is possible today." The time has come, Foner boldly asserts, "to reintroduce integration into our political vocabulary—not as a code for whites dictating to blacks or as 'color-blindness,' a term appropriated from the civil rights movement by conservatives and made into an empty slogan, but as a vision of a nation transformed, one in which equality is a reality for all Americans." It was a goal that Foner and I tried to pursue further in a special issue of *The Nation* that we co-edited, titled "Reclaiming Integration."

In the penultimate entry in this anthology, "Letter to Bernie," from November 2015, Foner praises Senator Bernie Sanders for having "energized and inspired millions of Americans and forced the questions of economic inequality and excessive corporate power to the center of our political discourse." He also makes a suggestion, however, about the way progressives ought to try to persuade their neighbors to pursue a different, more egalitarian path. His counsel is rooted, unsurprisingly, in his study of American history. Foner maintains that the next time the senator or any other "democratic socialist" is asked to explain his ideological commitments, he or she should point not to traditions abroad, fine though they may be, but to the American radical tradition—Frederick Douglass and Abby Kelley, Eugene V. Debs and A. Philip Randolph, Betty Friedan and Martin Luther King Jr. "[T]alk about our radical forebears here in the United States," Foner advises, "for the most successful [domestic] radicals have always spoken the language

of American society and appealed to some of its deepest values."
Good contemporary progressive politics, Foner insists, requires a
solid knowledge of the American radical tradition.

* * *

At its best, *The Nation* features informed, creative, inspiring writing
that speaks to current affairs with a gravity and a prescience that
rewards close and careful reading. Foner's work meets that standard. Pieces he wrote decades ago can profitably be studied today.
His retrospective in 1977 on the lethal hounding of Nicola Sacco
and Bartolomeo Vanzetti is tragically resonant in our own moment
of hysteria over immigration and terrorism. Reflections he penned
in the 1990s on the politics of memorialization make for useful
reading now, as people and institutions across the country grapple
with how we ought to remember our past. His eloquent declaration
in the aftermath of 9/11 is an assertion that will undoubtedly remain
vital as long as there is a United States: "At times of crisis the most
patriotic act of all is the unyielding defense of civil liberties, the
right to dissent and equality before the law for all Americans."

The Nation at its best also fosters progressive pluralism:
a community in which there exists respectful contentiousness.
Foner's writings mirror productive controversies within the
American left at large. Much of the writing about race found in the
pages of *The Nation* over the past several decades bears the imprint
of a black separatist sensibility that Foner explicitly challenges in
championing his conception of integration. He does not denounce
or demean the separatist sensibility. Far from it: he lauds some
of its most impressive proponents, including, most importantly,

W.E.B. Du Bois (a figure for whom Foner repeatedly and elaborately expresses admiration and gratitude). Yet he ultimately disagrees with important facets of the Black Power tradition that has become so popular among many racial justice activists. Similarly, regarding struggles over public memory, Foner differs with some progressives who want to tear down all memorials to figures who were white supremacists. Instead, he advances a strategy of addition rather than subtraction, declaring that "statues of black Civil War soldiers, slave rebels, civil rights activists and the like should share public space with Confederate generals and Klansmen, all of them part of America's history." Neither *The Nation* nor Foner is afraid of contestation, including disagreements among comrades and allies. Both, however, are keenly attuned to the opportunistic inconsistencies of reactionary ideological enemies. "Americans applauded the Muscovites who ... toppled the statue of Felix Dzerzhinsky, founder of the Soviet secret police," Foner observes, before noting the sour irony that "citizens of New Orleans who demanded the removal of the monument glorifying the [racist] White League were denounced as 'Stalinists' by a leading historian in the pages of the *New York Times*."

* * *

I end on a personal note. I met Eric Foner in 1976 when he was a visiting professor at Princeton University and have been in close touch with him ever since. He has been an unfailingly gracious and helpful mentor. My happy experience as a beneficiary of his generosity has been replicated many times over in the lives of undergraduates, professional peers and, perhaps most tellingly, his graduate students.

No living historian has reaped more professional recognition. Foner's first book, *Free Soil, Free Labor, Free Men: The Ideology of the Republican Party Before the Civil War*, remains after nearly half a century the standard treatment of its subject (attracting the enthusiastic appreciation even of Karl Rove!). *Reconstruction: America's Unfinished Revolution, 1863–1877* won the Bancroft Prize, the Francis Parkman Prize, the Avery O. Craven Prize, the Lionel Trilling Prize and the Los Angeles Book Award. *The Fiery Trial: Abraham Lincoln and American Slavery* won the Pulitzer Prize, the Bancroft Prize and the Lincoln Prize. Foner has served as president of both the Organization of American Historians and the American Historical Society. He has been awarded many honorary degrees (e.g. Dartmouth and Princeton) and has been inducted into various organizations (e.g. the British Academy and the American Academy of Arts and Sciences).

Given all the acclaim, falling into self-importance would be easy, indeed, difficult to avoid. But Foner is free of pretentiousness. He is an earnest educator who seizes upon whatever forum is available to share his knowledge and insight. His success has sporadically attracted envy and resentment and his steadfast fidelity to progressive aspirations has occasionally attracted red-baiting and accusations of anti-Americanism. Foner, however, has refrained from pursuing personal vendettas and ideological vilification, another reason he enjoys tremendous and widespread admiration.

Finally, it should be noted that in the most intimate sphere of his life, Foner has conducted himself in a fashion that is also instructive and uplifting. He is a loving family man dedicated to his wife, the distinguished historian of dance Lynn Garafola, and his daughter, Daria Foner, a graduate student in art history. I am lucky to be his friend and am grateful for having had the opportunity to read him over the years, in his books and in the pages of *The Nation*. ❖

The Men and the Symbols

AUGUST 20, 1977

*My conviction is that I have suffered for things that
I am guilty of. I am suffering because I am a radical
and indeed I am a radical; I have suffered because
I was an Italian, and indeed I am an Italian.*
—Bartolomeo Vanzetti, 1927

I t is fifty years this month since two immigrant Italians,
Nicola Sacco and Bartolomeo Vanzetti, died in the electric chair in Massachusetts. Yet "the case that will not die"
still arouses emotional controversy and remains a pivotal
event in the history of American justice. It will continue to do so,
not only because of the character of the two men but because, as
Edmund Wilson wrote at the time, the case "revealed the whole
anatomy of American life, with all its classes, professions and
points of view and all their relations, and it raised almost every
fundamental question of our political and social system."

In origin, Sacco and Vanzetti were no different from the millions of other immigrants who entered the United States early in this century. Sacco was born in the village of Torremaggiore in southeastern Italy, one of seventeen children in a relatively prosperous peasant family. Emigrating to this country in 1908 at the age of 17, he learned to edge-trim shoes and worked in a shoe factory in Milford, Massachusetts. The common picture of Sacco as a "good shoemaker," suggesting the familiar Italian-American cobbler, is misleading; he was a skilled factory workman who commanded high wages. By the time of his arrest in 1920 he was married, owned a house and had accumulated $1,500 in savings.

In contrast to Sacco, the settled family man, Vanzetti was an itinerant, unskilled laborer, one of the innumerable "tramps" and migrants of the period who could not or would not adjust to the discipline of the new industrial order. Born in northwestern Italy in 1888, he had spent seven years in school and later took great pride in recalling his excellent record. Arriving in America in 1908, he was first a dishwasher in New York City restaurants, then roamed New England, working variously in a stone quarry, a brick furnace, digging ditches and finally as a fish peddler.

Neither man had come to America as a radical, but both were attracted to anarchism here. Sacco and his wife on occasion performed in street theater to raise funds for the anarchists, and both men were involved in strikes and war resistance. Sacco collected bread for the Lawrence strikers in 1912 and assisted strikes of Massachusetts foundry and shoe workers; Vanzetti was blacklisted for his part in a strike at a Plymouth cordage factory in 1916.

When the two men met is not known. However, in 1917 Sacco, Vanzetti and other New England anarchists fled to Mexico for a year to avoid the draft and possible deportation for antiwar activities. The more intellectual of the two, Vanzetti, during his years in America read books ranging from Dante to Marx, Tolstoy and Kropotkin. Both lived among Italians, neither spoke English well and both planned to return to Italy. It was their arrest that made them fully a part of American life.

I

The crime with which Sacco and Vanzetti were charged and the conduct of their trial have been recounted many times, but it is probably well to summarize them briefly. On April 15, 1920, a shoe company in South Braintree, Massachusetts, was the scene of a robbery and murder. As a paymaster and guard carried the $16,000 payroll to the factory, two men who had been waiting nearby shot and killed them, and were then picked up by a car carrying three other men. Sacco and Vanzetti were arrested three weeks later while accompanying Mike Boda, an anarchist friend suspected of involvement in the crime, to pick up his car from a repair shop.

At their trial, a major issue was made of the fact that Sacco and Vanzetti were armed at the time of their arrest and lied under initial questioning, denying knowing Boda or being anarchists. This behavior, according to the prosecution, revealed a "consciousness of guilt." Since at the time they had not been told of the charges against them, it seems plausible to assume that the guilt of which they were conscious was radicalism, not robbery. They lied to protect their friends and associates, as well as to avoid possible deportation.

The arrests coincided with the period of the most intense political repression in American history. During World War I the Espionage and Sedition Acts had made illegal virtually any utterance against the war. With the war's end, the foreign-born radical replaced the savage Hun as the symbol of evil for self-appointed defenders of the American way. The postwar Red scare culminated in the notorious Palmer raids of January 1920, when 4,000 radicals were rounded up and several hundred eventually deported.

Sacco and Vanzetti knew, moreover, that the police were less than scrupulous in their treatment of arrested anarchists. Vanzetti had just been to New York, where he had investigated the two-month detention of the Italian anarchist Andrea Salsedo. After Vanzetti's return to Plymouth, two days before his arrest, Salsedo plunged fifteen stories to his death from the offices where he was being questioned by federal agents.

The trial of Sacco and Vanzetti for the South Braintree crime opened on May 31, 1921. The prosecution sought to place the two at the scene through eyewitnesses and a few pieces of physical evidence; the defense produced eyewitnesses who denied that either man had been there, and others to establish alibis.

The evidence against Vanzetti was absurdly thin. Only one man claimed to have seen him at the scene of the crime, and he identified Vanzetti as the driver of the getaway car, contradicting almost all other witnesses, who described the driver as of fair complexion. The prosecution also claimed, with little supporting evidence, that the .38 revolver Vanzetti was carrying at the time of his arrest belonged to the murdered guard. The defense produced thirteen witnesses, all Italian, to testify that Vanzetti had been selling fish on the day of the crime.

Regarding Sacco, there was eyewitness testimony that he had and had not been at the scene. Some prosecution witnesses, in violation of standard police procedure, had viewed Sacco individually instead of in a lineup, whereupon their initial recollection of the murderer's physical appearance improved remarkably. Others claimed, implausibly, that Sacco had spoken to them in clear, unaccented, colloquial English.

The key testimony against Sacco was the assertion that the .32 bullet found in the body of the guard had been fired from the revolver Sacco had on him when arrested. Each side produced ballistics experts to affirm or deny the claim. The prosecution expert, Capt. William Proctor of the State Police, testified that the bullet was "consistent with" having been fired from Sacco's gun. He later admitted that the prosecution had carefully coached him in that exact wording after he had said he could not make a positive identification. He added that he did not believe Sacco's gun had fired the shot. In 1961, two experts commissioned by Francis Russell, the author of *Tragedy in Dedham: The Story of the Sacco-Vanzetti Case* (1962), reaffirmed the theory that Sacco had fired the fatal shot, a conclusion that remains in dispute.

To accept the controversial ballistics evidence, one must not only dismiss Sacco's alibi but also ignore all the gaps in the prosecution's case. Sacco claimed to have gone to Boston that day to obtain a passport for return to Italy. The defense produced witnesses from the Italian Consulate, others who had lunched with him in Boston, and a man who recognized Sacco as having sat across from him on the train. More important, perhaps, is the evidence the prosecution did not present. No attempt was made to determine who had fired five of the six bullets found in the bodies of the dead men, to link the defendants with the stolen money, to establish a motive for the crime, or to present fingerprints as evidence, even though newspaper reports indicated fingerprints had been found on the getaway car.

The entire trial, moreover, was conducted in an atmosphere of intense hostility to the defendants. Seasoned newspaper reporters were shocked by the blatant prejudice shown by Judge Webster Thayer, and by prosecutor Frederick Katzmann's sarcastic, bullying cross-examination of the defendants as to their political beliefs. With Sacco, Katzmann raised such questions as whether he loved America, whether America was a free country, why he had avoided the draft, what he thought of Harvard University, and whether he sent his son to public school (he did). Thayer later remarked to a friend. "Did you see what I did with those anarchistic bastards?"

In such an environment, a conviction was a foregone conclusion. For six years defense lawyers filed successive motions for a new trial, pleading new evidence, recantation of prosecution witnesses, the prejudice of the judge, and a confession implicating the Morelli gang of Providence, Rhode Island, in the robbery. But Judge Thayer rejected all motions and in 1926 the Massachusetts Supreme Court upheld his decision.

Finally, in the spring of 1927, Thayer pronounced a sentence of death. By this time, the case had become an international *cause célèbre*. Governor Fuller appointed a three-member advisory commission to consider the fairness of the verdict. Consisting of Samuel Stratton, president of M.I.T.; Robert Grant, a former judge; and, at the head, Abbott Lawrence Lowell, president of Harvard, the commission was an embodiment of Brahmin respectability. As *The New Republic* observed, "The life of an Italian anarchist was as foreign to them as life on Mars." Lowell's presence recalled the turbulent history of the immigrant factory workers in the cities bearing his familial names. For years he had been an official of the Immigration Restriction League; among his contributions to life at Harvard was the establishment of a segregated residence for black students. The commission's findings affirmed the verdict and sentence, and, despite last-minute appeals to the federal courts, Sacco and Vanzetti were executed. "What more can the immigrants from Italy expect?" remarked Heywood Broun. "It is not every prisoner who has a president of Harvard throw on the switch for him."

II

In her account of the August days preceding the execution, Jeanette Marks observed, "Already as individuals Nicola Sacco and Bartolomeo Vanzetti were being lost sight of … already they had gone from our midst … [they had become] symbolic." The sentimental portrait of a humble shoemaker and fish peddler had, even before their deaths, begun to obscure the living persons. Nowhere is this more apparent than in the way writers on the case have treated the anarchism of Sacco and Vanzetti. Perhaps the problem can be stated as follows: everyone recognizes the importance of politics in the case, but most writers refuse to take the politics of the two men seriously. Herbert Ehrmann, one of the defense lawyers, found their political views "absurd and pathetically impracticable." Francis Russell, who believes Sacco was guilty, considers their beliefs "nobly absurd." Roberta Feuerlicht, the latest student of the case, who is convinced both were innocent, speaks of Vanzetti "prattling about the proletariat" and finds anarchism so senseless that she is "skeptical how deep their beliefs ran." In fact, anarchism was central to the lives of both men.

Today, when anarchists represent a minor fringe in most countries, it is perhaps difficult to recall that before World War I the militant left in Europe and America tended to be anarchist. Within a span of twenty years anarchists assassinated the monarchs of Italy and Austria-Hungary, the presidents of France and the United States, and the prime minister of Spain. In this country, ever since the Haymarket affair of 1886, the image of the bomb-carrying anarchist evoked the kind of fear Bolshevism would inspire in a later decade. "For half a century," as John Dos Passos wrote in 1927, "anarchy has been the bogy of American schoolmasters, policemen, old maids and small-town mayors."

The United States has had two distinct anarchist traditions. Native anarchism, symbolized by Emerson and Thoreau and deriving from the distrust of government so pervasive in the writings of

Paine and Jefferson, was a form of extreme individualism. It was often coupled with pacifism or nonviolence and usually coexisted with a commitment to private property as the bulwark of individual freedom. Immigrant anarchism, associated first with Germans, then Italians, was, in contrast, a form of libertarian communism. As Errico Malatesta, the great Italian anarchist, put it, "anarchy without socialism is impossible."

The millennial dream of Italian anarchism was a communal society in which the triad of Old World evils—state, church and private property—had been abolished. More than in any other country, anarchists in Italy exalted the "propaganda of the deed." Terrorism, sabotage and assassination were all considered legitimate ways to stir the masses to revolutionary fervor. "We are all revolutionaries," said Malatesta, "because we believe that only the revolution, the violent revolution, can solve the social question."

Although anarchists comprised only a small part of the Italian left before World War I, through emigration they exerted a powerful influence on the anarchist movement abroad. Among the most important exponents of Italian anarchism in America was Luigi Galleani, the man Vanzetti acknowledged as "our master." A brilliant propagandist and polemicist, Galleani preached a stern brand of anarcho-communism, rejecting any form of political organization and advocating violent revolution and a relentless war against capitalism. In his newspaper, *Cronaca Sovversiva*, Galleani lionized McKinley's assassin Czolgosz as well as Gaetano Bresci, who had returned from Paterson, New Jersey, to assassinate King Umberto of Italy.

During World War I the federal government suppressed Galleani's newspaper when it urged Italians to resist the draft. Galleani himself was deported in May 1919, but not before he had called on his followers for violent revenge. Soon afterward bombs exploded in eight cities, and an Italian was killed trying to place a bomb at Attorney General Palmer's Washington home.

* * *

The little-studied Italian anarchist movement forms the backdrop for an understanding of Sacco and Vanzetti, who seem to have been members of one of the loosely organized groups of followers of Galleani that existed in Boston, New York, Paterson and other cities in those years. This does not prove, as Francis Russell claims, that Sacco "felt justified in committing even acts of robbery and murder for his cause." Most anarchists made a clear distinction between ordinary crime and acts of political violence; as Vanzetti later said, most of his political activity consisted of "talking on street corners to scorning men." But the point to remember is that, though Sacco and Vanzetti may never have committed violence, as followers of Galleani they were hardly the innocuous dreamers so often pictured in the literature on the case.

Most of what we know of the beliefs of the two men derives from their famous prison letters. Both were taught to read and write English in prison by wealthy New England women who had interested themselves in the case, and Vanzetti, in particular, became a highly articulate writer in English whose letters still evoke an emotional response. (The same is true of his Italian letters to his family, only portions of which have been translated.)

Sacco emerges from his prison letters as a man of sensitivity who was distraught over the prolonged separation from his wife and children and the inability to practice his craft. Yet the letters also reveal a social outlook underpinned by an unbending class consciousness and a view of himself and Vanzetti as "the good soldiers of the revolution."

Sacco's reputation for creative thought has suffered by comparison with Vanzetti's. But he was well acquainted with the anarchist press, including Galleani's newspaper, and at the time of his arrest had several dozen books in his home. Although he had received no formal schooling in Italy, he was hardly an illiterate. Nonetheless, events, not books, turned him toward anarchy. His experiences in the bitter strikes that wracked the ring of industrial towns around Boston affected his political outlook: in his letters there is little about the evils of government but much on the class struggle and the need for revolution. "I know," he told Judge Thayer, "the sentence will be between two classes, the oppressed and the rich class, and there will always be collision between one and the other."

Even in the personal letters expressing his grief at the separation from his family, Sacco moves instinctively from an individual to a collective point of view. He tells his daughter Ines how he wishes he could "see you running, laughing, crying and singing through the verdant fields," but then adds, "the same I have wished for other poor girls ... the nightmare of the lower classes saddened very badly your father's soul."

Contemporaries and historians have usually found Vanzetti the more attractive figure. While Sacco has been portrayed as dogmatic and proletarian, Vanzetti has been idealized as a philosophical dreamer. Even Elizabeth Gurley Flynn, active in the defense from the beginning, described Vanzetti's social outlook as simply "a belief in human freedom and the dignity of man. ... He would have been at home with Emerson, Henry D. Thoreau or Walt Whitman." Admirers dubbed Vanzetti a "philosophic anarchist," a phrase which Dos Passos translates as "an anarchist who shaves daily, has good manners and is guaranteed not to act on his beliefs."

"Philosophic anarchist" fails, however, to convey the depth of Vanzetti's anarchist convictions or the vision he shared with Sacco of being men of action within an ongoing radical movement. He had read extraordinarily widely and since 1914 had boarded in the Plymouth home of Vincenzo Brini, a stopping place for such anarchists as Galleani and Carlo Tresca. In prison, Vanzetti spent much of his time writing articles for *L'Asunata dei Reffratari*, a New York anarchist newspaper established by Galleani's followers in 1922. One series was titled "In Defense of the Revolution," another was a critique of syndicalism, yet another evaluated Soviet society from an anarchist point of view. He also translated anarchist literature into English. In other words, Vanzetti continued to take part in the ongoing debate about revolutionary tactics and politics within the anarchist movement. His political views did not differ significantly from those of other Italian anarchists.

Vanzetti has sometimes been portrayed as an American-style individualist. "The now-obsolete term anarchist-Communist would never have applied to Vanzetti," writes Russell. G. Louis Joughin and Edmund Morgan, authors of one of the most extensive studies of the case (*The Legacy of Sacco and Vanzetti*, published in 1948), declare that Vanzetti "rejects collectivism." Vanzetti, in fact, referred to himself precisely as an "anarchist-Communist." "We are Socialists," he wrote of himself and Sacco in 1927. "The difference—the fundamental one—between us and all the other is, that they are authoritarian while we are libertarian." Like Sacco, Vanzetti had an acute awareness of class distinctions. He wrote a criticism of the Beards' *Rise of American Civilization* remarkable in prefiguring more recent historical perceptions. "Nothing I found in it ... of the instinctive and intuitive aspirations of the poor, of the hardly articulated but incommensurable souls of the humbles —except if I believe that they are like the master..."

Vanzetti, then, was more than a simple "humanitarian" and hardly an individualist. It is true, however, that his anarchism did seem to undergo a process of Americanization in prison. Receiving the works of Emerson and Thoreau as gifts from his benefactors, Vanzetti as time went on began to play down the role of violence in anarchism. When in 1927 he petitioned Governor Fuller, affirming his innocence, Vanzetti could refer to Emerson's essays as a more complete exposition of his views.

A follower of Emerson was easier to defend in the Massachusetts of 1927 than a disciple of Galleani. But the partial Americanization of Vanzetti's anarchism was symptomatic of a larger ambivalence that affected his self-perception as the years went by. Sacco always held himself at a certain distance from their wealthy supporters or "philanthropists," as he called them. He told Gardner Jackson, "although knowing that we are one heart, unfortunately, we represent two opposite classes."

Vanzetti, by contrast, thrived on the attentions of the upper-class women who showered him with letters and gifts. One psychologist has suggested that the defense committee women played the role of Vanzetti's "American mothers." His own mother had died when he was 20 and his grief was inordinate. Vanzetti is not known to have shown an interest in women in America. "Oh friend," he wrote in 1923, "the anarchism is as beauty as a woman for me..."

Whatever the dynamics of his relationship to the defense committee women, Vanzetti was dazzled by his prolonged exposure to the upper class. He was even flattered by Elizabeth Evans's offer to hire him as a gardener upon his release from prison. More important, he imbibed their unflagging belief that justice would eventually prevail. Sacco never shared this optimism and after the sentencing withdrew entirely from the appeals effort. Vanzetti was caught up in the role of philosopher-in-the-rough; Sacco refused to play the part marked out for him. Perhaps he instinctively understood that by transforming them into symbols, the larger audience was losing sight of both their individuality and their convictions.

III

In her new memoir on the case (*The Never-Ending Wrong*) Katherine Anne Porter recalls the August days in Boston when writers and intellectuals took part in the campaign to save Sacco and Vanzetti from the electric chair. Inadvertently, she gives the impression that intellectuals were the only ones who did so.

There is no question that by the time of the executions, an impressive array of American writers had lent their services to the defense. Aside from Porter, one thinks of John Dos Passos, H.L. Mencken, Heywood Broun, Edna St. Vincent Millay and Dorothy Parker, as well as others less directly involved, including John Dewey and Jane Addams. Such writers and thinkers discovered in the case a personal and political cause that transcended the alienation of the 1920s, when some writers expatriated themselves to Europe and many others retreated into a domestic exile.

The presence of the intellectuals in Boston helped attract world attention to the final act of the drama and was a significant episode in the history of the intellectual community. In point of fact, however, Mencken and Dos Passos were the only writers of reputation involved in the case before 1927. Dos Passos identified with Sacco and Vanzetti because of his own intellectual affinity for anarchism and because as a Harvard student his name had led to his being treated as "a wop or a guinea or a greaser."

Much of our understanding of the case comes from the writings of intellectuals who, not surprisingly, exaggerated their own importance. Granville Hicks wrote at the time, "The battle was between the intellectuals and everybody else." In terms of publicity, however, the labor movement carried the burden. Even before the trial, unions in Boston and the surrounding mill towns had protested the arrests, and by 1927 a dozen state labor federations and the AFL national convention had demanded a new trial.

Locals of the United Mine Workers and ILGWU were especially active in fundraising, and in 1927, here as abroad, the majority of demonstrations were sponsored by labor organizations.

The degree of labor activity was the more remarkable because of the division and retreat of the labor movement in the 1920s. A decade of reaction followed the false dawn of 1919, when Communist revolutions were attempted in Germany and Hungary, general strikes took place in Winnipeg and Belfast, and this country experienced the great steel strike and countless other militant labor disputes. Union membership declined by more than a million in the 1920s. From today's vantage point the decade appears as a watershed in modern American history, a time of declining resistance to the emerging corporate order. New departments of employee psychology sought to mold the working class in the employers' image, while in the press, pulpit and pay packets, in speeches at factory gates by patriots dressed as Uncle Sam, workers were reminded that socialism and trade unions were un-American.

IV

If labor's contribution to the defense has been neglected, the involvement of the Italian-American community and the effect of the execution upon it have been virtually ignored. From the outset a tightly knit group of Italian anarchists organized the defense committee, and Italian-Americans provided the money to keep it afloat. Most of the $300,000 that had been raised by the end of 1926 came in small donations from working people, a majority of them Italian, and from such organizations as the Lega Antifascista of Pittsburgh and the Brooklyn Italian-American Democratic Club. The case created a remarkable unity in Italian America; even the pro-Fascist Italian press of New York City supported the two men, much to Vanzetti's discomfort.

In 1927 Italian labor leaders in New York City sought to organize a nationwide general strike of protest, the respectable Sons of Italy sent a massive petition to Governor Fuller, and 20,000 representatives of labor unions and Italian fraternal organizations marched in Philadelphia on July 4. On the famous days when Katherine Anne Porter was arrested for picketing in Boston (when Porter "did not see anyone identifiably a working-man") the majority of the picketers were foreign born.

To Dos Passos, Sacco and Vanzetti were "all the immigrants who have built this nation's industries with their sweat and their blood and have gotten for it nothing." To Italian America and, by extension, to the larger immigrant community, they represented all the Italian immigrants victimized by the stereotypes of Italians as knife-wielding criminals who lived by the code of the vendetta. A prominent legal scholar, Dean John Wigmore of Northwestern University Law School, could link the two men with, among other things, "the thugs of India, the Camorra of Naples, the Black Hand of Sicily."

Hovering over the Italian-American community in the 1920s was the cloud of Fascism, which had devastating effects on the Italian-American left. But that community was also under assault from the massive drive to homogenize American culture.

The xenophobia of the postwar years was reflected in its most extreme form in the revival of the Ku Klux Klan; but also in the ending of unrestricted immigration. More generally, it could be seen in the involvement of schools, churches, civic organizations and corporations in the Americanization movement. That movement had reached its peak during World War I, when it became the justification for suppressing dissent; but as part of the effort to integrate the immigrant working class into an ordered, homogeneous society it persisted into the 1920s.

To the immigrants, as one Italian-American editor put it, "Americanization is an ugly word." Dos Passos was bitterly, ironically on target when he subtitled his pamphlet on the case "Story of the Americanization of Two Foreignborn Workmen." It was no accident that the Veterans of Foreign Wars chose Americanization Day (April 27, 1927) for a vigorous attack on Sacco and Vanzetti. The two men symbolized the alien threat to provincial, Anglo-Saxon America.

For the Italian-American left, the execution was one of a series of spiritual blows, beginning with the deportations of 1919-20 and the triumph of Mussolini, from which the movement never really recovered. To the majority of Italian-Americans, it seemed self-evident that the men were persecuted because they were Italian; this was the bond that united Italian immigrants of all political views in their defense. The executions, following a decade of persecution, strengthened the insularity of an already apolitical community, which had brought across the Atlantic an instinctive distrust of law, police and the state.

After all, despite the labor and intellectual allies of the two men, it did seem that the executions reflected the popular will, at least in Massachusetts. "Respectable Boston is possessed with the lust to kill," wrote Mike Gold in his angry piece, "Lynchers in Frockcoats." But if it was a lynching, much of the community was implicated. The defenders of Sacco and Vanzetti were astonished by the vehemence with which the cab drivers, shop clerks and subway guards of Boston—except in the Italian North End—supported the execution of the "damn Reds." How symbolic that James M. Curley, the Irish boss of Boston, denounced Sacco and Vanzetti at the Bunker Hill celebration in 1927. Anglo-Saxon and Irish Boston seemed to have united against the two men, and the isolation of the Italians could not have been more complete.

Porter, in an account which perhaps reflects something of the intellectuals' attitude toward Boston's Italians, recalls a rally in which a "raging crowd" of Italians, "howling like beasts," shouted their "childish phrases." "They'll pay, they'll pay," the crowd cried in Italian. When the bodies lay in state in the North End, one bouquet of flowers bore a ribbon with the motto, "*Aspettando l'ore di vendetta*"—"Awaiting the hour of vengeance." But there was no vengeance, and ten years later, to Italian-Americans like Vito Marcantonio, their death was "still an open wound in the hearts of many of us." The case politicized some Italian-Americans, like the young lawyer Michael Musmanno, but it drove many more back into the privacy of their family and community. Francis Russell, who hounded Sacco's son Dante for some statement of his father's innocence, interpreted Dante's silence as a tacit admission of guilt.

But perhaps it reflected not only a desire to avoid publicity but a distrust of all outsiders that the case had accentuated throughout Italian America.

For many intellectuals, the execution was equally traumatic. As Edmund Wilson said, it "made the liberals lose their bearings." Nothing since World War I so shook the liberal faith in the workings of American institutions or the self-sufficiency of the rule of law. The case was a prelude to the leftward turn of many intellectuals in the 1930s. Most notable, perhaps, was Dos Passos, for whom the case provided the conception of America as two nations, the artistic scaffolding of *U.S.A.*, his prose-poem of class warfare.

To Italians it was obvious, in the old Mezzogiorno maxim, that "the law works against the people." Sacco always assumed that the legal system would afford a radical no justice, and Vanzetti, despite his optimism, was convinced as an anarchist that "the laws are the codified will of the dominating classes." But the intellectuals and many on the defense committee simply could not believe the executions would take place. This was Massachusetts, after all, not some Southern state where legal and extralegal lynchings were a matter of course. Therefore, "the catastrophe that nobody had really believed would happen," as Malcolm Cowley described the execution, was devastating when it came.

For Felix Frankfurter, who did more than any individual to rally respectable opinion behind the two men, the case was a test of the rule of law itself. What disturbed Frankfurter, then teaching at Harvard Law School, was not so much an erroneous verdict and a prejudiced trial—hardly unusual occurrences—but the approval of the outcome by the legal profession and the courts. The organized bar considered criticism of the case tantamount to treason—a view, Frankfurter insisted, that could only "work a lasting damage to confidence in our whole system of law."

A true conservative, Frankfurter knew the executions would undermine respect for the law. His young associate, Sidney Glueck, put it another way: "Will [the case] even bring about a fundamental change in that sinister, cynical logic of our craft which will persist in the confusion of means and end, in the raising of law above justice?"

Glueck had hit on one of the fundamental issues to arise from the case. In a thoughtful piece in the May issue of *Harper's*, Professor Sanford Levinson has observed how the notion of "rule of law" is often casually invoked, as if the concept were self-evidently benevolent, and as if it had anything necessarily to do with "justice." Actually the rule of law was upheld in the Sacco-Vanzetti case. The appeals process was pursued from the local level all the way to the Supreme Court, and at each step appellate judges made decisions fully in accord, with precedent. The "great dissenter," Supreme Court Justice Oliver Wendell Holmes, not only refused to stay the executions but would not even read the evidence in the case, "except on the limited points that came before me." The rule of law was vindicated but, in the words of the armband worn by the mourners, "justice [was] crucified."

The day of their death, August 23, 1927, would remain a mental benchmark for millions of Americans of that generation, just as the death of Roosevelt and the assassination of Kennedy would be for their children and grandchildren. Some would remember Sacco and Vanzetti for their bearing in the final days, for the dignity and courage they personified. To others, they would simply be two innocent victims, men whose individuality was dwarfed by the larger injustices they came to symbolize. But we should also think of them as rebels, men of action, dreamers of a perfect world where, as Vanzetti wrote, humanity could move beyond "a cursed past in which man was wolf to the man." Sacco and Vanzetti went to their deaths convinced that the outcome would only speed the victory of their cause: "that agony is our triumph." Perhaps the tragedy of their case lies not only in the injustice that was done but in the fact that their execution was one in a long train of events that seems to have driven their utopian vision out of American life. ❖

The Televised Past

JUNE 16, 1979

A few weeks ago, I spent three days in California attending a conference devoted to the docudrama, that blend of fact and fiction now so much in vogue on television. Among the fifty-odd participants were such TV heavyweights as David Susskind and *Roots* producer David Wolper, along with a host of writers, directors and network executives. There were also a few TV critics and a number of outside stars such as Gore Vidal (who angered his audience by announcing that he never watches television), along with four historians of rather more modest fame.

Like the rest of television programming, docudramas run the gamut from serious drama to soap opera, but most begin with the laudable intention of illuminating an aspect of the past. Some of these, like two shows re-creating the Entebbe raid, are thrown together with a haste mirrored in the shoddiness of the productions. Others, like *The Adams Chronicles* or the dramatization of Watergate, John Dean's *Blind Ambition*, are high-budget affairs, thoroughly researched and years in the making.

Collision Course: Truman and MacArthur and *The Ordeal of Patty Hearst* typify, each in its own way, shows that deal with real people in real situations. Others, like *Holocaust*, portray fictional characters in a historical setting.

Obviously, the mingling of fact and fiction, history and drama, is nothing new. What is new is not the docudrama form itself but the insistent claims for historical authenticity that accompany it and the controversy these claims have aroused. Sharp criticism of the genre has appeared in the pages of *TV Guide*, the *New York Times*, *Saturday Review* and other publications. The docudrama form has been accused of allowing fiction to masquerade as history, of allowing writers to play fast and loose with the facts while retaining the veneer of historical authenticity. The critics are alarmed by what they perceive as distorted history reaching the huge audience commanded by television.

Not only TV critics but network executives, too, are uneasy over the recent flood of docudramas. In particular, they are alarmed by a vulnerability to litigation arising from ambiguities in the law governing privacy, publicity and defamation of character. A docudrama on the Scottsboro case resulted in an unsuccessful lawsuit by one of the surviving white women in the trial. CBS settled out of court with the former wife of blacklisted newsman John Henry Faulk, who objected to her portrayal in *Fear on Trial*.

* * *

Despite quibbling by the critics and occasional lawsuits, docudramas are big business. Their ratings range from the spectacular success of *Roots* to the disaster of *King*, but most do significantly better than the average series. Moreover, television people believe that the claim of historical authenticity is especially important for promotion. Although historical fiction is a time-honored genre, networks, producers and writers all resist the notion that docudramas should be labeled and thought of in this way. The claim of truth, according to one executive, means ten extra ratings points, an important consideration at a time of the fiercest ratings war in television history.

It is interesting that many docudrama producers are ex-documentary makers who blend their respect for "reality" with an affinity for the larger audiences and freedom to invent that are afforded by the docudrama. As one producer told the conference, "I used to film the outside of the White House and wonder what was going on in the Oval Office. Now I can imagine it." Thus, like the term "docudrama" itself, practitioners of the art are somewhat schizophrenic. They want the creative freedom of the artist but also the imprimatur of the historian, an air of authenticity without the full responsibility that goes along with it.

Despite these inherent problems, docudramas like *Roots* are in a class of their own when compared with what passes for prime-time TV entertainment. Historians, moreover, should be grateful that, at a time of declining enrollment in college and high school history courses, the docudrama boom reveals a broad receptivity to historical subject matter. Much of the interest in televised history is simply voyeurism, a video exposé of the secret lives of historical celebrities. But the better shows not only present compelling explorations of historical themes, they challenge the historical profession to respond creatively to the mass audience for history reflected, and stimulated, in successful docudrama.

Nonetheless, it is not surprising that many historians look askance at this particular gift horse. For the history presented is, almost inevitably, distorted. Compared with film, the medium of television seems to demand a smaller scale—close-ups, small groups, scaled-down sound—in its presentation of historical events. It is hardly surprising then that in so many docudramas, the dramatic space is reduced to a single focus: a historical personage, a famous courtroom trial, a family.

But the fact that individual action is highlighted and collective action ignored is not simply a consequence of the small screen. Even more, one suspects, it reflects the persistent hold of that peculiarly American strand of individualism on the writers. In *Roots: The Next Generations*, for example—possibly the finest exploration of the black experience ever presented on television— political and economic forces are transformed into personal ones. Blacks are disenfranchised because a few white leaders stand to gain from it; black sharecroppers get their AAA benefits not by organizing a sharecroppers' union but through the intervention of Alex Haley's father. *King* made the black revolution the work of one man, *Tail Gunner Joe* made McCarthyism the product of a single somewhat deranged individual. If "the personal is political" was the slogan of the 1960s, docudramas seem to assume that the political is unfailingly personal.

Nonetheless, no one can claim that television is presenting a sugarcoated version of history. *Roots*, both the first and second parts, was a powerful indictment of American racism. Audiences have been treated to extremely unfavorable portraits of McCarthyism (*Tail Gunner Joe* and *Fear on Trial*), a harrowing account of the detention of Japanese-Americans (*Farewell to Manzanar*), and the suppression of the American Indians (*I Will Fight No More Forever*). Several projects dealing with Vietnam are being prepared, and while NBC recently killed a proposed docudrama on the Pueblo Indians, ABC is dramatizing our home-grown holocaust, the experience of the Creeks and Cherokees in the Trail of Tears.

Although many of the assembled writers and producers at the conference insisted that there can be a docudrama without a point of view, or, in good positivist fashion, that an interpretation emerges inductively from the mass of material gathered for the production, television is, in fact, presenting a coherent vision of America's past. Recent docudramas are consolidating and validating for a mass audience the revisionist view of this country's domestic history that gained currency among historians in the 1960s and is now broadly accepted in the academic world and increasingly incorporated into American history textbooks. This revisionist literature, a reaction against the bland "consensus" history of the 1950s and a response to the rise of black consciousness in the 1960s, portrays American history as filled with group conflict, racial injustice and threats to democratic institutions.

Television's point of view seems firmly ensconced within this revisionist consensus. Nor does it venture beyond it, either to the left or to the right. It is difficult to imagine the networks dramatizing Watergate from Richard Nixon's point of view, just as I do not expect to see a docudrama on Eugene V. Debs and the old Socialist Party. Also, TV history is only selectively revisionist. If racial injustice is an acceptable subject, class conflict is not. The history of American labor is ignored in the docudrama, as is the experience of the immigrant. The fiftieth anniversary of the execution of Sacco and Vanzetti, the occasion of extensive coverage on French and Italian TV, passed unmarked by the American networks, including PBS.

Nor has television proved particularly adventurous in dealing with foreign policy. A docudrama on the Cuban missile crisis of 1962 virtually canonized John F. Kennedy, and the same approach characterized *Truman at Potsdam*. The revisionist portrait of Roosevelt and Truman as deeply implicated in the origins of the Cold War has yet to appear on the TV screen. Aside from Nixon, in fact, twentieth-century presidents tend to be treated with kid gloves. The recently aired *Ike* did portray Winston Churchill as being more interested in confronting the Russians than in rescuing France from Nazi occupation during World War II, but it suggested that Roosevelt and Eisenhower would have none of this "politicization" of the war effort. In *Backstairs at the White House*, a succession of modern presidents are presented as thoroughly apolitical individuals, inoffensive and rather congenial, except for Warren Harding who, we are told, had a drinking problem and an eye for beautiful women.

Television, moreover, seems distinctly uncomfortable with historical material that does not have a finite ending. The ratings failure of *King* is widely attributed to its "depressing" denouement —the assassination and the program's suggestion that the racial problem remains with us. How much more uplifting to view *Roots*, "the triumph of an American family." Some of the emphasis on docudrama may, in fact, reflect an escape from contemporary social issues into the past. Even Watergate is almost noncontroversial seven years after the break-in; like the Vietnam War, it seems safely behind us and, thus, safe for television.

Another reflection of TV's flight from current problems, and one of the lamentable side effects of the docudrama craze, has been the virtual banishment of the documentary from network television. This is especially unfortunate since, by contrast to docudrama, the straightforward documentary has a clearly delineated structure of factual content. Its focus on issues rather than personal drama seems far better able to present the complexities of history and of current affairs.

Many current issues, however, are considered by television simply too hot to handle. First and foremost are those for which large and vocal pressure groups exist. Don't expect to see a show dealing with abortion or gun control on the air anytime soon. Or, as one reporter asked at the conference, "What have you done on the oil companies lately?" Even historians can be a pressure group, although their effectiveness has yet to be determined. The announcement that CBS is considering a production based on Jefferson's purported relationship with his slave Sally Hemings has elicited a furious response from the self-appointed guardians of our third president's reputation.

Even more important than a fear of controversy in explaining the demise of the documentary are the almighty ratings, a consideration never far from the surface in any discussion of TV programming. Executives, writers and producers are unanimous in one conviction: "No one watches documentaries." (Of course, "no one," in this context, may mean 20 million people.) As Art Buchwald observed, the motto of the conference might have been, "Whether you are a producer, director, writer or historian, you have a right to make a buck."

This conclusion may be harsh, but it does point up a problem left unresolved at the docudrama conference. The writers and producers are being pulled simultaneously in three directions by the claims of drama, history and finance. If the marriage of history and drama is difficult, that of art and industry is even more so.

The fact is, however, that these docudramas *are* teaching history. My students' conception of slavery is more likely to come from *Roots*, their picture of McCarthyism from *Tail Gunner Joe*, than from the monographs I and my colleagues write. But given the present structure of the television industry, it seems unlikely that, however outstanding individual productions may be, television can fully live up to its potential for illuminating the American past. ❖

The Romance of the Market

For four months last spring, I taught American history at Moscow State University and, with my wife and 2-year-old daughter, braved the ever-increasing difficulties of daily life in the city. Over the years, many visitors to the Soviet Union have arrived with a fully formed mental image and have seen what they came to see. This was not our experience.

We came to Moscow expecting to find a society reveling in new-found intellectual openness and engaged in an exciting debate over its future. We soon discovered, however, that the early euphoria of *glasnost* had faded. Now, the public mood is one of cynicism about the past and present coupled with deep pessimism about the future. Instead of a spirited, multisided discussion of the country's economic and political restructuring, we found a political situation oddly reminiscent of America's: genuine freedom of speech but little real difference of opinion in public discussion.

On television, in the newspapers and in private conversations (at least among the academic, intellectual and artistic circles in which we traveled), praise of the "free market" is universal. Debate centers on the pace of change, not its direction. Those who voice doubts about the benefits of the impending "market revolution" are dismissed as representatives of the "old thinking." In 1917, as John Reed noted in *Ten Days That Shook the World*, the Bolsheviks' appeal lay partly in the fact that at a time of crisis, they alone had "a constructive programme." Today, so fully have advocates of the free market captured the intellectual initiative that no one seems capable of advancing an analysis of the economic crisis or a plan for dealing with it within an explicitly socialist framework.

Ironically, the romance of the market arises as much from the successes of Soviet socialism as from its all-too-apparent failures. Karl Marx expected capitalism to give birth to its gravedigger—an exploited, class-conscious proletariat. In fact, socialism has sown its own seeds of discontent by wrenching the USSR, at tremendous cost, from backwardness to modernity and by creating, almost from nothing, a vast class of professionals, intellectuals and white-collar workers.

These academics, journalists, artists, scientists and managers stand at the cutting edge of demands for economic change. Unlike their counterparts of an earlier generation, who measured in their own lives how far the Soviet Union had traveled from the widespread illiteracy and social misery of czarist days, this generation compares its conditions of life with the contemporary West. Thanks to *glasnost*, thousands of them have traveled abroad for the first time. And coupled with the crisis of the Soviet economy, their encounter with the Western standard of living has been a shattering experience. To remind such people that not all Americans share in capitalism's bounty is beside the point. They are interested in their own equivalents overseas, not the plight of the poor or the homeless.

This intelligentsia and managerial class—those the Western press calls "radicals" or "democrats"—are the most insistent advocates of far-reaching economic and political change. In the USSR, these terms carry different meanings than they do in the West. Soviet radicals admire Margaret Thatcher, Milton Friedman and the virtues of unfettered capitalism. Each week *Moscow News*, among the most influential radical journals, contains articles that would comfortably find a home in publications of the Heritage Foundation or the American Enterprise Institute.

One piece blamed America's economic problems on labor unions, whose exorbitant wage demands supposedly rendered some industries, like steel and autos, uncompetitive. Another praised General Pinochet for introducing "overdue" economic changes to Chile. According to *Moscow News*, not only should state-owned enterprises be privatized but public welfare spending should be cut to the bone. "The state budget," one article insisted, "cannot take care of everyone. They must protect themselves by earning what they can and using the new conditions of the market economy."

Soviet democrats are more interested in the structure of government—an independent judiciary and multiparty legislature to act as checks against absolutism—than in a politically engaged citizenry. Indeed, they fear the popular will as an obstacle to economic change, and they are not certain that in a democratic system the radical intelligentsia would, in fact, prevail.

Gavriil Popov, the newly elected Mayor of Moscow and a man associated with both free-market reform and political democratization, recently pointed out that these two goals are in some sense mutually contradictory. The "tasks that must be carried out"— that is, the restoration of capitalism—will, Popov wrote in the *New York Review of Books*, produce greater and greater economic inequality. That, in turn, will stimulate political disaffection. Popov's solution was not to cushion the inegalitarian impact of the market economy but to speed up economic change before popular opposition has time to coalesce.

"The masses," wrote Popov, "long for fairness and economic equality." This deeply ingrained popular attitude is perhaps Soviet socialism's most enduring intellectual legacy. It goes hand in hand with suspicion of suddenly acquired wealth, widespread distaste for the naked greed now rampant in black-market and hard-currency dealings, a widespread preference for rationing of scarce goods as opposed to raising prices, and a staunch commitment to maintaining the USSR's fraying but still extensive social "safety net."

American journalists periodically have a field day citing belief in equality and suspicion of entrepreneurship as evidence of the innate backwardness of the "Russian character." To Soviet radicals, those attitudes seem a pernicious legacy of seventy years of Communism. As of today, anti-market sentiments have failed to find organized political expression. But they certainly worry free-market advocates.

This past spring both the opposition and the official press were filled with articles criticizing equality as an archaic notion, hopelessly out of date in the late twentieth century.

Indeed, a new "crime" has lately been added to the list of Stalin's perfidies: By narrowing wage differentials between the skilled and the unskilled, and between professional and manual workers, he promoted the idea of equality. (In fact, Stalin presided over a steady retreat from wage equality, but it is fashionable today to blame him for every conceivable ill of Soviet society, including those for which he bore no responsibility.)

At first glance, the romance of the market seems to rest on an admixture of naïveté and wishful thinking. The current obsession with uncovering the Soviet Union's hidden history coexists with a remarkable historical amnesia, or ignorance, regarding the West. The radicals assume that the Western standard of living has arisen naturally from the functioning of capitalism; they condemn the very union movement and popular struggles that helped create today's high income levels and mass-consumption societies.

In language reminiscent of our own "end of ideology" theo-rists of the 1950s, Soviet radicals insist that ideology itself has been discredited, that politics ought to be guided by "common sense," without considering that the idea of the free market is itself ideological. They call for a pragmatic approach to politics, an end to social experiments, and in the same breath propose a transformation of Soviet society every bit as utopian as the orig-inal revolution. They have no sense of capitalism and the market as global systems within which, to put it mildly, standards of living vary enormously, and in which the exploitation of Guatemalan peasants or Mexican migrant laborers has something to do with the abundance of fruits and vegetables in American supermarkets.

Yet the widespread appeal of market ideology cannot be attributed simply to self-deception or tunnel vision. Writing about the eighteenth century, the historian Franco Venturi called equality a "protest ideal." It was less a blueprint for change than a criticism of existing society. The market plays the same role in today's Soviet Union.

Despite their belief in equality and their fear of the price increases, unemployment and social dislocation certain to follow in the wake of radical economic reforms, many ordinary Russians find themselves attracted to the idea of the free market. This is not only because it promises a cornucopia of consumer goods (or at least basic items from socks, aspirin and snowsuits to condoms, all of which had disappeared from the shelves by the time we arrived in Moscow). In listening to Russians fascinated with the market's magical qualities, I felt as if I was being transported back to debates at the dawn of modern capitalism.

More than a decade ago, in writing a book about Thomas Paine, I was puzzled by his enthusiastic embrace of the laissez-faire ideology of Adam Smith. Only gradually did I come to understand the profoundly liberating implications of market ideology in the eighteenth century. Opposition to government control of the economy dovetailed with hostility to powerful institutions resting on inherited privilege: the established church, closed corporations, a hereditary monarchy and aristocracy. To men like Paine, the free market was a democratic innovation in a society in which status rested not on individual merit but on one's place in a complex web of privilege and patronage.

In today's USSR, it is not simply the ubiquitous shortages but how people do manage to obtain things that feeds discontent. In a world of empty stores, shopping is commonly done through the back door—that is, via bribes, barter and official or family connections. Even those in a position to benefit from this system find it unfair and humiliating. To a large extent, whom you know now determines your standard of living. There is something positively egalitarian about the way money in a market society can erase other social distinctions, about a world in which anybody with the cash can walk into a store and purchase whatever goods he or she pleases, without incurring personal obligations.

Thus popular opinion in the Soviet Union appears poised between fear of the inequalities of a market society and resentment over the inequities daily encountered in the burdensome task of putting a meal on the table. In this situation, it seems unlikely that a coherent alternative to the free-market agenda will develop any time soon. ✤

Fighting for the West
(written with Jon Wiener)

JULY 29, 1991

"The West as America: Reinterpreting Images of the Frontier, 1820-1920," an exhibit at the Smithsonian Institution's National Museum of American Art, has become the latest target in the assault on "politically correct" thought by longtime conservatives, onetime radicals and academics enamored of campus life before the advent of large numbers of women and minority students. Critics accusing this show of being "PC" have once again wrapped themselves in the mantle of intellectual liberalism while accusing their opponents of political indoctrination and thought control. But at the Smithsonian, as on most college campuses, abuses inspired by political correctness remain a minor problem. Their significance is dwarfed by the myriad real crises in university and cultural life—among them dwindling public funds, rising corporate influence, the fragmentation of scholarship and widespread illiteracy. "Political correctness" ranks with the swine flu epidemic and comet Kohoutek as molehills transformed into mountains by a gullible media. The Smithsonian controversy suggests that it is the right, not the left, that today poses the real threat to intellectual freedom.

Senator Ted Stevens, the Alaska Republican, made the Smithsonian show a national issue in a Senate Appropriations Committee hearing in May, when he accused the museum of advancing a leftist political agenda and threatened to cut the institution's budget in retaliation. "You're in for a battle," he told Smithsonian officials. Washington Republican Senator Slade Gorton echoed the charge. (Stevens later acknowledged that he had not, in fact, seen the show. What prompted his crusade was a well-publicized remark by former Librarian of Congress Daniel Boorstin in the museum's comment book that the exhibit was "perverse, historically inaccurate, [and] destructive.")

The press quickly entered the fray. The *Washington Post*'s Ken Ringle called the show "the most cynical exhibit … ever presented under the aegis of your tax dollars and mine." The *New York Times*'s senior art critic, Michael Kimmelman, blasted the show's "simplistic" and "forced" analyses. The wildest attack came from political columnist Charles Krauthammer: The exhibit, he wrote, had "a crude half-baked Marxist meanness"; it could have appeared "thirty years ago in Moscow."

Those who actually visit "The West as America" may well be disappointed to discover that the exhibit is decidedly unscandalous. It begins with a seemingly unexceptional premise: that nineteenth-century paintings do not simply record Western "reality." Instead, as a wall label states, they are "products of convention" rooted in the dominant ideologies of their time. Of course, placing the work of artists in historical context is hardly a new idea. What the critics object to is the nature of the historical interpretation presented in tandem with these particular works of art.

In most assaults on "political correctness," the bogyman is "multiculturalism"—the movement to expand subjects like history and literature to include the experiences of previously neglected groups. Critics of "The West as America," however, are after larger game—nothing less than an entire interpretation of the American past. What they want is the kind of relentlessly celebratory account of American development so common in the 1950s. To Krauthammer, the show expresses "contempt for every achievement of Western expansion"; the *Post*'s Ringle complained that the show "trashes ... most of our national history."

Scholars may be excused for finding this somewhat tendentious. As Patricia Nelson Limerick of the University of Colorado at Boulder, a leading historian of the West, puts it, "This show is about as revolutionary as if you had a Southern history exhibit, hung romantic paintings of plantations, and then said slavery was a rough business—not a very wild proposition, and the same kind of proposition this show offers about the West."

Limerick, of course, knows full well that a heroic vision of the West retains a powerful hold on the American imagination. She and others founded the "New Western History," which has transformed our understanding of the region over the past decade or so. These scholars have hammered the final nail into the coffin of Frederick Jackson Turner's "frontier thesis," which saw westward expansion as a mystical social process in which European culture was stripped away by settlers' encounter with nature. On the frontier emerged the quintessential American, cut free from the European past and devoted to individualism, democracy and equality.

In the New Western History, the West is not a process but a place—a place inhabited by people, not just nature, and fought over by a multiethnic cast of characters including Easterners, Mexicans, Native Americans and blacks. The conquest of the West is a story of success and failure, heroism and betrayal, capitalist triumph and labor exploitation. Colorado miners and Mexican peons are as much a part of the story as pioneers on the Oregon Trail. In other words, the West's development was a complex history, not a simple heroic progress.

Howard Lamar, the Yale historian whose work inspired much of this new history, writes in the exhibition catalogue that the West has always been "a place to project wishes and dreams," and that in so doing, Americans "reveal themselves and their own ideologies." American history contained many Wests, all more or less "invented," all different from the prosaic and intermittently violent reality of white settlement and Native American dispossession. At the Constitutional Convention, Madison argued that the West could save America from Old World class conflict. Half a century later Horace Greeley saw it as a safety valve for oppressed Eastern workers. The doctrine of Manifest Destiny held that the West would fulfill America's divinely ordained role as savior of the world. Economic writers often viewed the West as a passage to India, a route by which America could dominate trade with the Far East. Today, it seems, the New World Order requires a West free of exploitation, racism and other inconvenient realities of American life.

* * *

That the West has always existed in the imagination as much as in reality is the theme of the Smithsonian show. The *Washington Post* declared it "curious" that "the art and the arguments of the show's organizers tend to operate at cross-purposes." But that is precisely the show's message. The nineteenth- and early twentieth-century paintings on display celebrated the conquest of the West. The accompanying wall labels challenge viewers not to take the paintings at face value, but to reinterpret them in terms of what historians have come to understand about Western expansion.

The show emphasizes that artists painted the West to conform to the expectations of Easterners, especially wealthy patrons of the arts and railroad companies interested in promoting Western settlement and tourism. Easterners wanted to see a West more honest and clean, more stirring and uplifting, than their own troubled region, suffering in the late nineteenth century from periodic depressions and violent class conflict. The paintings promised settlers a peaceful journey to fertile lands, and the artists paid special attention to "the triumphs of engineering"— railroads, bridges, etc. The wall texts take note of what the paintings left out: abandoned homesteads and mining towns that went bust; social conflict and environmental damage.

Often, artists portrayed the West as if it was entirely uninhabited. When they did depict Native Americans, much of their work tended to be stereotypical. The exhibition section "Inventing the Indian" has turned out to be one of the most controversial. These paintings, the much-maligned wall text declares, "tell more about the feelings and ideas of artists and patrons than about the 'Indians' whose lives they represent." Early in the nineteenth century, Native Americans were portrayed as noble savages; later, as they were being driven off their land, they were portrayed as violent aggressors (even though they were usually the victims of aggression). Later still, the "doomed Indian" (representing the fantasy that the whole problem might be eliminated by Indians simply dying out) and the acculturated Indian became prominent themes.

The final room, on early twentieth-century painters, also aroused considerable ire. One guide who has taken groups around the museum reported that while many visitors accept the idea that paintings of Indians are not entirely "accurate," they nevertheless become irate when presented with the idea that the West may not have "really" been the way Frederic Remington painted it.

Nor do they appreciate being confronted by Remington's racism. "Jews—inguns—chinamen—Italians—Huns—" he wrote, were "the rubish of the earth I hate." In the same letter to a friend, he boasted, "I've got some Winchesters and when the massacre-ing begins … I can get my share of 'em and whats more I will." It does not seem entirely farfetched to speculate, as the wall text does, that Remington's painting *Fight for the Water Hole*, in which some tough-looking Texans defend themselves from Comanche attack, may have been colored by these prejudices. And when the work is placed in the context in which it was painted—America in 1903, thirty years after the event it portrayed—it can be viewed as an allegory in which a native-born white elite is surrounded by menacing and uncivilized immigrants. But Krauthammer ridiculed those interpretations, describing the painting as simply "a classic cowboys vs. Indians gunfight," and the *Washington Post*'s Ringle approvingly quoted an assertion that it portrays nothing more or less than "the truth ... basic reportage."

The Captive, by Irving Couse (Wikicommons)

Critics also objected to the museum's interpretation of *The Captive*, by Irving Couse, which portrays a helpless young white woman in a flowing white dress, her hands and feet tied, lying unconscious at the feet of an Indian warrior, who quietly stares at her. The wall text suggests that the painting expresses white culture's "fears of miscegenation," which aroused a storm of protest from, among others, the *New York Times* and *Newsweek*, both of which ran reproductions of the painting. The warrior's arrows, on the ground, point at the helpless woman, suggesting a sinister version of Cupid; the catalogue interpreted the arrows as phallic symbols, an idea critics dismissed with contempt.

The painting's sexual imagery is ambiguous, but the critics seem most offended not by the museum's Freudianism (hardly a new idea, even in Stevens's Alaska) but by any effort to interpret a work of art. Krauthammer's argument that Remington painted only "a classic cowboys vs. Indians gunfight" falls into this category. This view reveals the deep strain of anti-intellectualism and provincialism that lies just beneath the surface of the assault on "political correctness."

Some of the show's wall texts are, indeed, didactic—a common failing in museum prose—but the critics are upset by its substance, not just its style. Rather than criticism, however, the exhibition curators deserve praise for the extensive archival work that has enabled them to place these mostly mediocre and forgotten paintings in a historical context. The show includes Henry Farny's 1902 portrait of Ogallala Fire in full warrior regalia. However, as Alex Nemerov's catalogue essay reports, Ogallala Fire was at that time not a warrior on the plains but a janitor in the Cincinnati Art Club. "The hand that erstwhile wielded the tomahawk and scalping knife now handles the broom and dustpan," Farny wrote.

What the catalogue calls "the hopeless separation of Western artists from the era they sought to document" was evident in other cases. A revealing photo of Charles Schreyvogel at work shows him at his easel, in front of a cowboy who crouches as he aims his revolver. They are on the roof of an apartment building in Hoboken, New Jersey, in 1903. Schreyvogel actually went to Colorado to sketch Pike's Peak in 1911; he wrote home to his wife, "I started [sketching] with Pike's Peak in the back ground and it looked fine. I was there at 7:30 a.m. Then the smelters started in and the black smoke just covered the whole valley so that I couldn't see a thing and had to stop." Of course, in his paintings the Western landscape always appears luminous and pristine—a West of the imagination rather than reality.

* * *

Although Senators Stevens and Gorton, and many Eastern critics, are outraged by the New Western History, in the West itself the regional political establishment has a different view. Increasingly, it welcomes the new history for its emphasis on the region's diversity of peoples and experiences. The Western Governors' Association invited Limerick and other practitioners of the new history to speak at their conference last summer and has published a collection of essays on new ways of looking at the region's past, *Beyond the Mythic West*. (The first essay was written by former Secretary of the Interior Stewart Udall.) "Inside the beltway is a special place," Limerick argues, "a place where Western senators dress up as quaint prospectors. But if that exhibit had come to Denver it would get nowhere near the amount of whining it did in D.C."

"The West as America," however, will not travel to Denver. Previously scheduled appearances at the art museums there and in St. Louis have now been canceled. Both museums plead a shortage of funds rather than fear of controversy, but surely if the exhibit had received the praise it deserved rather than a politically inspired assault, money would have been found to bring the show west.

Despite fears that "The West as America" reflects yet another takeover of a cultural institution by 1960s radicals, Senator Stevens can rest assured that the Smithsonian is no hotbed of political correctness. Most of the exhibitions in its complex of museums are thoroughly conventional. The National Air and Space Museum is nothing more than a celebration of American greatness; it must warm Professor Boorstin's heart. In the Ceremonial Court of the National Museum of American History, the visitor can view ball gowns of the last seven first ladies—with no embarrassing mention of the scandal over Nancy Reagan's requisitioning of hundreds of thousands of dollars' worth of "gifts" from the world's top designers. Nearby is a display of presidential memorabilia: Wilson's golf clubs, Cleveland's trout flies, Harding's riding crop; no Freudian interpretation, no historical context, no mention of Wilson's Red Scare, Cleveland's economic depression or Harding's sexual escapades; just a reliquary.

Indeed, critics of "The West as America" will be delighted to find in the National Museum of American History the show "Westward to Promontory," presenting photos of the building of the transcontinental railroad. Here, the labels are wholly celebratory of "the great enterprise of the nineteenth century." The theme is the triumph of capitalism and the reknitting of the post–Civil War Union, with barely a mention of exploited Chinese laborers or dispossessed Indians, and none at all of the struggle over Reconstruction taking place at the same time.

The Smithsonian, according to one staff member who preferred to remain anonymous, is "the most reactionary place I've ever been. It's anything but liberal." Nonetheless, Stevens's threats have had a chilling effect on an already conservative institution. Curators have changed some of the wall texts for "The West as America" to soften the impact. The changes have not been extensive—five rewritten labels and five new ones out of a total of fifty-five, according to exhibition curator William Truettner. Many of the changes were made in the section "Inventing the Indian." One label no longer states that Indians were considered "racially and culturally inferior." Apparently in response to the complaint that the show has nothing good to say about the paintings, another now credits them with "valuable ethnographic detail."

Truettner insists that the changes were planned before Stevens launched his assault—although they were not executed until the controversy began. He admits that curators in the future will have to be more "careful" about labels that may offend powerful interests. His observation is reinforced by reports from other Smithsonian employees, speaking off the record, that labels for future shows are being edited to avoid provoking right-wing senators or the White House.

Another example of the chill emanating from Stevens's office can be found at the Hirshhorn Museum, which took the unusual step of posting a warning that visitors "may find disturbing" some of the work in the Awards in the Visual Arts exhibit that opened there in June. The Hirshhorn is part of the Smithsonian, and its curators worried especially about a piece by Adrian Piper depicting a lynching. A museum spokesperson said the warning was posted because of the "climate," which the *Washington Post* took to be a reference to Stevens's threat.

* * *

The attack on "The West as America" comes after the *New Republic, Newsweek, Time, New York* magazine and others have blasted away at the campus left, portraying it as "thought police" out to destroy intellectual freedom. Dinesh D'Souza's *Illiberal Education* has reached the bestseller list, arguing as Roger Kimball did in a similar book that "tenured radicals" now control the universities and suppress freedom of speech with tactics that "border on the totalitarian." President Bush himself recently joined the chorus. These laments, however, ring a bit hollow when one reflects that none of these self-proclaimed opponents of censorship have uttered a word of protest against a senator's threat to cut the Smithsonian budget because he dislikes an exhibition's interpretation of American history.

The Smithsonian, it seems certain, will ride out this storm, but the controversy over "The West as America" is a harbinger of more trouble to come. The museum world, like academia, has lately been changing in ways many conservatives find deeply threatening. Long devoted simply to collecting and displaying memorabilia of prominent men and emblems of American greatness, museums are now seeking to present a more complex, diversified and critical portrait of the American past.

The Chicago Historical Society, for example, recently dismantled its Lincoln Gallery, complete with his top hat, ice skate and pieces of wood from his log cabin, and replaced it with an exhibit emphasizing the centrality of slavery and racism in nineteenth-century American history. Richmond's Valentine Museum currently displays a pioneering exhibition on "Jim Crow: Racism and Reaction in the New South." The Museum of the Confederacy in Richmond recently opened a major show on slavery, a far cry from its usual preoccupation with Robert E. Lee, Stonewall Jackson and the Lost Cause.

"The West as America" is part of this development and represents a significant achievement for the Museum of American Art. We need more shows like this—exhibits that bring forgotten paintings back to life as documents of social and cultural history. Since most of these mediocre genre paintings and banal landscapes long ago lost their status as art, today they are viewed by few people outside the Buffalo Bill Historical Center or the Cowboy Hall of Fame. This exhibition has given us a new way to see them: as images that convey white Americans' obsessive preoccupation with their country's virtue. The Smithsonian, unfortunately, now plans to close this show July 28; it's too bad it can't remain open longer.

All these new exhibits offend some viewers, who go to museums for "old-fashioned" history. But they are appreciated by many others. At "The West as America," the visitors' comment book is filled with perceptive remarks; not everyone wants an exhibit about the West where never is heard a discouraging word. "Where's the paintings the Indians did of the whites?" asks one visitor, a legitimate question. Some comments are sharply critical, but more are rather favorable. "This exhibit," one visitor wrote, "helps me think about the art, the artists, the patrons, the audience, the subjects. Thanks." Is it possible that ordinary people actually appreciate being challenged by new ideas? Senator Stevens, please take note. ❖

The Education of
Richard Hofstadter

MAY 4, 1992

T he relationship between politics and intellectual life, at the center of today's debate over "political correctness," multiculturalism and other real and imagined sins of the academy, is hardly a new phenomenon. Throughout our history, contemporary political problems and commitments have shaped the questions Americans asked about their past and the answers they found. The career of Richard Hofstadter, the finest historian of his generation, offers a case in point. The reissue of his first book, *Social Darwinism in American Thought*, provides an opportunity to consider Hofstadter's own intellectual trajectory and some of the influences that molded American scholarship of the eras of the Great Depression and Cold War.

Richard Hofstadter was born in 1916 in Buffalo, New York, the son of a Jewish father and a mother of German Lutheran descent. After graduating from high school in 1933, he entered the University of Buffalo, where he majored in philosophy and minored in history. As for so many others of his generation, his formative intellectual and political experience was the Great Depression. Buffalo, a major industrial center, was particularly hard hit by unemployment and social dislocation. The Depression, Hofstadter later recalled, "started me thinking about the world. ... It was as clear as day that something had to change. You had to decide, in the first instance, whether you were a Marxist or an American liberal." At the university, Hofstadter gravitated toward a group of left-wing students, including the brilliant and "sometimes overpowering" (as Alfred Kazin later described her) Felice Swados, read Marx and Lenin, and joined the Young Communist League.

In 1936, on the eve of his graduation, Hofstadter and Felice were married, and subsequently they moved to New York. Felice first worked for the National Maritime Union and International Ladies' Garment Workers Union and then took a job as a copy editor at *Time*, while Hofstadter enrolled in the graduate history program at Columbia University. Both became part of New York's broad radical political culture that centered on the Communist Party in the era of the Popular Front. Hofstadter would later describe himself (with some exaggeration) as "by temperament quite conservative and timid and acquiescent," and it seems that the dynamic Felice, a committed political activist, animated their engagement with radicalism. Nonetheless, politics for Hofstadter was much more than a passing fancy; he identified himself as a Marxist, and in apartment discussions and in his correspondence with Felice's brother Harvey Swados, he took part in the doctrinal debates among Communists, Trotskyists and others that flourished in the world of New York's radical intelligentsia.

In 1938, Hofstadter joined the Communist Party's unit at Columbia. The decision, taken with some reluctance (he had already startled some of his friends by concluding that the Moscow purge trials were "phony"), reflected a craving for decisive action after "the hours I have spent jawing about the thing." As he explained to his brother-in-law: "I join without enthusiasm but with a sense of obligation. ... My fundamental reason for joining is that I don't like capitalism and want to get rid of it. I am tired of talking. ... The party is making a very profound contribution to the radicalization of the American people. ... I prefer to go along with it now."

Hofstadter, however, did not prove to be a very committed party member. He found meetings "dull" and chafed at what he considered the party's intellectual regimentation. By February 1939 he had "quietly eased myself out." His break became irreversible in September, after the announcement of the Nazi-Soviet pact. There followed a rapid and deep disillusionment—with the party (run by "glorified clerks"), with the Soviet Union ("essentially undemocratic") and eventually with Marxism itself. Yet for some years Hofstadter continued to regard himself as a radical. "I hate capitalism and everything that goes with it," he wrote Harvey Swados soon after leaving the party. Never again, however, would he devote his energies in any sustained manner to a political cause. He became more and more preoccupied with the thought that intellectuals were unlikely to find a comfortable home in any socialist society likely to emerge in his lifetime. "People like us," he wrote, "have become permanently alienated from the spirit of revolutionary movements. ... We are not the beneficiaries of capitalism, but we will not be the beneficiaries of the socialism of the 20th century. We are the people with no place to go."

Although Hofstadter abandoned active politics after 1939, his earliest work as a historian reflected his continuing intellectual engagement with radicalism. His Columbia master's thesis, written in 1938, dealt with the plight of Southern sharecroppers, a contemporary problem that had become the focus of intense organizing efforts by Socialists and Communists. Hofstadter showed how the benefits of New Deal agricultural policies in the cotton states flowed to large landowners, while the sharecroppers' conditions only worsened. The essay presented a devastating indictment of the Roosevelt administration for pandering to the South's undemocratic elite. Its critical evaluation of Roosevelt, a common attitude among New York radicals, would persist in Hofstadter's writings long after the political impulse that inspired the thesis had faded.

As with many others who came of age in the 1930s, Hofstadter's general intellectual approach was framed by Marxism, but in application to the American past, the iconoclastic materialism of Charles Beard was his greatest inspiration. "Beard was really the exciting influence on me," Hofstadter later remarked. Beard taught that American history had been shaped by the struggle of competing economic groups, primarily farmers, industrialists

and workers. Underlying the clashing rhetoric of political leaders lay naked self-interest; the Civil War, for example, should be
understood essentially as a transfer of political power from
Southern agrarians to Northern capitalists. Differences over the tariff
had more to do with the war's origins than did the debate over
slavery. Hofstadter's first published essay, a "Note" in a 1938
issue of the *American Historical Review*, took issue with Beard's
emphasis on the tariff as a basic cause of the Civil War while
accepting the premise that economic self-interest lay at the root
of political behavior. (The homestead issue, Hofstadter argued,
far outweighed the tariff as a source of sectional tension.) The
article inaugurated a dialogue with the Beardian tradition that
shaped much of Hofstadter's subsequent career.

While Beard devoted little attention to political ideas, see-
ing them as mere masks for economic self-interest, Hofstadter
soon became attracted to the study of American social thought.
His interest was encouraged by Merle Curti, a Marxist Columbia
professor with whom Hofstadter had formed, according to
Felice, a "mutual admiration society." Other than his relationship
with Curti, however, Hofstadter was not particularly happy at
Columbia. For three years running, he was refused financial aid.
Hofstadter was gripped by a sense of unfair treatment. "The guys
who got the fellowships," he complained, "are little shits who
never accomplished or published anything." (None of them, one
can assume, had, like Hofstadter, published in the *AHR*).

Denied financial aid, Hofstadter was forced to seek a teaching
job. In the spring of 1940, he obtained a part-time position in the

evening session of Brooklyn College. His first full-time job was at the downtown branch of City College, where a position opened in the spring of 1941 because of the forced departure of a professor accused of membership in the Communist Party. The New York legislature's Rapp-Coudert Committee had been investigating "subversive" influences within the city colleges; eventually, some forty teachers were fired or forced to resign after being named by informants. Students initially boycotted Hofstadter's lectures as a show of support for his purged predecessor, but eventually they returned to the classroom. Ironically, Hofstadter's first full-time job resulted from the flourishing of the kind of political paranoia that he would later lament in his historical writings.

Meanwhile, having passed his comprehensive examinations, Hofstadter set out in quest of a dissertation topic. With Curti's approval, he settled on social Darwinism. By mid-1940, he was hard at work, and two years later, at the precocious age of 26, he completed the dissertation. *Social Darwinism in American Thought* was published by the University of Pennsylvania Press in 1944.

Social Darwinism was the perfect subject for the young Hofstadter. It was a big topic, likely to interest a large audience, and it combined his growing interest in the history of social thought with his continuing alienation from American capitalism. It was the kind of subject, Felice wrote Harvey, "in which all his friends want to have a hand." "But in which they won't," Hofstadter added. The book focuses on the late nineteenth century and ends in 1915, the year before Hofstadter's birth. But, as he later observed, the "emotional resonances" that shaped his approach to the subject were those of his own youth, when conservatives used arguments descended from social Darwinism to justify resistance to radical political movements and government efforts to alleviate inequality. Studying social Darwinism helped explain "the disparity between our official individualism and the bitter facts of life as anyone could see them during the great depression."

Social Darwinism in American Thought describes the broad impact on intellectual life of the scientific writings of Charles Darwin and the growing use of such Darwinian ideas as "natural selection," "survival of the fittest" and "the struggle for existence" to reinforce conservative, laissez-faire individualism. The book begins by tracing the conquest of Darwinian ideas among American scientists and liberal Protestant theologians, a conquest so complete that by the Gilded Age "every serious thinker felt obligated to reckon with" the implications of Darwin's writings. Hofstadter then examines the "vogue" of Herbert Spencer, the English philosopher who did more than any other individual to define nineteenth-century conservatism. Spencer, of course, preceded Darwin; well before the publication of *The Origin of Species*, Spencer not only coined the term "survival of the fittest" but developed a powerful critique of all forms of state interference with the "natural" workings of society, including regulation of business and public assistance to the poor. But Spencer's followers seized upon the authority of Darwin's work to claim scientific legitimacy for their outlook, and to press home the analogy between the natural and social worlds, both of which, they claimed, evolved according to natural laws.

Despite the book's title and the deftness with which he sketches the lineaments of social Darwinism in its opening chapters, Hofstadter actually devotes more attention to the theory's critics than its proponents. Beginning in the 1880s, social Darwinism came under attack from many sources—clergymen shocked by the inequities of the emerging industrial order and the harshness of unbridled competition, reformers proposing to unleash state activism in the service of social equality, and intellectuals of the emerging social sciences. Hofstadter makes no effort to disguise his distaste for the social Darwinists or his sympathy for the critics, especially the sociologists and philosophers who believed intellectuals could guide social progress (views extremely congenial to Hofstadter at the time he was writing). But Hofstadter's true heroes were the early twentieth-century Pragmatists. William James destroyed Spencer's hold on philosophical thought by insisting that human intelligence enabled people to alter their own environment, thus rendering pointless the analogy with nature—but James evinced little interest in current events. Hofstadter identified more closely with John Dewey, whom he presents as a model of the socially responsible intellectual, the architect of a "new collectivism" in which an activist state attempts to guide and improve society.

By the turn of the century, social Darwinism was in full retreat. But even as Darwinian individualism waned, Darwinian ideas continued to influence social thinking in other ways. Rather than individuals striving for advancement, the struggling units of the analogy with nature became collectives—especially nations and races. With the United States emerging as a world power after the Spanish-American War, writers like John Fiske and Albert Beveridge marshaled Darwinian ideas in the service of imperialism, to legitimate the worldwide subordination of "inferior" races to Anglo-Saxon hegemony. In the eugenics movement that flourished in the early years of the twentieth century, Darwinism helped to underwrite the idea that immigration of less "fit" peoples was lowering the standard of American intelligence. Fortunately, the "racist-military" phase of social Darwinism was as thoroughly discredited by World War I, when it seemed uncomfortably akin to German militarism, as conservative individualism had been by the attacks of progressive social scientists.

When Hofstadter tries to explain the rise and fall of social Darwinism, he falls back on the base-superstructure model shared by Marxists and Beardians in the 1930s. The reason for the ascendancy, until the 1890s, of individualist, laissez-faire Darwinism, Hofstadter writes, was that social Darwinism served the needs of those groups that controlled the "raw, aggressive, industrial society" of the Gilded Age. Spencer and the other social Darwinists were telling businessmen and political leaders what they wanted to hear. Subsequently, it was not merely the penetrating criticism of Lester Ward, John Dewey and others but the middle class's growing disenchantment with unbridled competition, Hofstadter argues, that led it to repudiate social Darwinism and adopt a more reform-minded social outlook in the Progressive era.

Actually, Hofstadter offered no independent analysis of either the structure of American society or the ideas of most businessmen or politicians. His effort to explain social Darwinism's rise and fall is a kind of *obiter dictum*, largely confined to his brief concluding chapter. Indeed, Hofstadter later reflected that the book may have inadvertently encouraged the "intellectualist fallacy" by exaggerating the impact of ideas without placing them in the social context from which they sprang. *Social Darwinism* is a work of intellectual history, not an examination of how ideas reflect economic structures. And as such, it retains much of its vitality half a century after it was written. The book's qualities would remain hallmarks of Hofstadter's subsequent writing—among them an amazing lucidity in presenting complex ideas, the ability to sprinkle his text with apt quotes that make precisely the right point, the capacity to bring past individuals to life in telling portraits.

Social Darwinism has had an impact matched by few books of its generation. Hofstadter did not invent the term social Darwinism, which originated in Europe in the 1860s and crossed the Atlantic in the early twentieth century. But before he wrote, it was used only on rare occasions; he made it a standard shorthand for a complex of late nineteenth-century ideas, a familiar part of the lexicon of social thought. The book demonstrates Hofstadter's ability, even in a dissertation, to move beyond the academic readership to address a broad general public. Since its appearance in a revised paperback edition in 1955 (Hofstadter left the argument unchanged but added an author's note and made several hundred "purely stylistic" alterations), it has sold more than 200,000 copies.

Inevitably, *Social Darwinism* now seems in some ways dated. Today, in the wake of the "new social history," historians are more cognizant of the many groups that make up American society and no longer write confidently, as Hofstadter did, of a single "public mind." Given the pervasive impact of literary deconstruction, it seems decidedly (perhaps refreshingly) old-fashioned to assume, with Hofstadter, that texts have a single, rationally ascertainable meaning. But the most striking difference between Hofstadter's cast of mind and that of our own time lies in his resolute conviction that social Darwinism was an unfortunate but thankfully closed chapter in the history of social thought. Hofstadter wrote from the certainty that social Darwinism was demonstrably wrong, that biological analogies are "utterly useless" in understanding human society, that this episode had all been some kind of "ghastly mistake."

"A resurgence of social Darwinism," Hofstadter did note, was "always a possibility so long as there is a strong element of predacity in society." But he could hardly have foreseen the resurrection in the 1980s of biological explanations for human development and of the social Darwinist mentality, if not the name itself: that government should not intervene to affect the "natural" workings of the economy, that the distribution of rewards within society reflects individual merit rather than historical circumstances, that the plight of the less fortunate, whether individuals or races, arises from their own failings. Had he lived to see social Darwinism's recrudescence, Hofstadter would certainly have noted how two previously distinct strands of this ideology have merged in today's conservatism—the laissez-faire individualism of a William Graham Sumner (who, it should be noted, condemned the imperial state with the same vigor he applied to government intervention in the economy) and the militarist and racist Darwinism of the early twentieth century.

This is not the occasion for an extensive survey of Hofstadter's subsequent career, but it may be useful to trace briefly how in later writings he both departed from and returned to the ideas expressed in his first book. If *Social Darwinism* announced Hofstadter as one of the most promising scholars of his generation, his second work, *The American Political Tradition*, published in 1948, propelled him to the very forefront of his profession. Since its appearance, this brilliant series of portraits of prominent Americans, from the Founding Fathers through Jackson, Lincoln and FDR, has been a standard work in both college and high school history classes and has been read by millions outside the academy. Hofstadter's insight was that virtually all his subjects held essentially the same underlying beliefs. Instead of persistent conflict (whether between agrarians and industrialists, capital and labor, or Democrats and Republicans), American history was characterized by broad agreement on fundamentals, particularly the virtues of individual liberty, private property and capitalist enterprise.

With its emphasis on the ways an ideological consensus had shaped American development, *The American Political Tradition* in many ways marked Hofstadter's break with the Beardian and Marxist traditions. Along with Daniel Boorstin's *The Genius of American Politics* and Louis Hartz's *The Liberal Tradition in America* (both published a few years afterward), Hofstadter's second book came to be seen as the foundation of the "consensus history" of the 1950s. But Hofstadter's writing never degenerated into the uncritical celebration of the American experience that characterized much "consensus" writing. As Arthur Schlesinger Jr. observed in a 1969 essay, there was a basic difference between *The American Political Tradition* and works like Boorstin's: "For Hofstadter [and, as Schlesinger might have added, Hartz] perceived the consensus from a radical perspective, from the outside, and deplored it; while Boorstin perceived it from the inside and celebrated it." As a courtesy, Schlesinger sent Hofstadter a draft of the essay. In the margin opposite this sentence, Hofstadter, who never felt entirely comfortable with the consensus label, scribbled, "Thank you."

Hofstadter had abandoned Beard's analysis of American development, but he retained his mentor's iconoclastic, debunking spirit. In Hofstadter's hands, Jefferson became a political chameleon, Jackson an exponent of liberal capitalism, Lincoln a mythmaker and Roosevelt a pragmatic opportunist. If the book has a hero, it is abolitionist Wendell Phillips, the only figure in *The American Political Tradition* never to hold political office. As in *Social Darwinism*, Hofstadter seemed to identify most of all with the engaged, reformist intellectual. It is indeed ironic that one of the most devastating indictments of American political culture ever written became the introduction to American history for two generations of students.

"All my books," Hofstadter wrote in the 1960s, "have been, in a certain sense, topical in their inspiration. That is to say, I have always begun with a concern with some present reality." His first two books, he went on, "refract the experiences of the depression era and the New Deal." In the 1950s a different "reality" shaped Hofstadter's writing—the Cold War and McCarthyism. Having remarried after the death of his first wife in 1945 and taught for several years at the University of Maryland, Hofstadter assumed a teaching position at Columbia and again found himself part of New York's intellectual world. But this was very different from the radical days of the 1930s. He had "grown a great deal more conservative in the past few years," Hofstadter wrote Merle Curti, then teaching at Wisconsin, in 1953. But unlike many New York intellectuals, including a number of his friends, Hofstadter never made a career of anti-communism. Nor did he embrace neoconservatism, join the Congress for Cultural Freedom or become an apologist for America's Cold War policies. He was repelled by McCarthyism (although he declined Curti's invitation to condemn publicly the firing of Communist professors at the University of Washington). After supporting with "immense enthusiasm" Adlai Stevenson's campaign for the White House in 1952, Hofstadter retreated altogether from politics. "I can no longer describe myself as a radical, though I don't consider myself to be a conservative either," he wrote Harvey Swados a decade after Stevenson's defeat. "I suppose the truth is, although my interests are still very political, I none the less have no politics."

What Hofstadter did have was a growing sense of the fragility of intellectual freedom and social comity. His next book was *The Development of Academic Freedom in the United States*, written in collaboration with his Columbia colleague Walter Metzger and published in 1955. As with other intellectuals, his sensibility was strongly reinforced by the Holocaust in Europe and the advent of McCarthyism at home. Hofstadter understood McCarthyism not as a thrust for political advantage among conservatives seeking to undo the legacy of the New Deal but as the outgrowth of a deepseated anti-intellectualism and provincialism in the American population. The result was to reinforce a distrust of mass politics that had been simmering ever since he left the Communist Party in 1939. Reared on the assumption that politics essentially reflects economic interest, he now became fascinated with alternative explanations of political conduct—status anxieties, irrational hatreds, paranoia. Influenced by the popularity of Freudianism among New York intellectuals of the 1950s and by his close friendships with the sociologist C. Wright Mills and literary critics Lionel Trilling and Alfred Kazin, Hofstadter became more and more sensitive to the importance of symbolic conduct, unconscious motivation and, as he wrote in *The Age of Reform* (1955), the "complexities in our history which our conventional images of the past have not yet caught."

Hofstadter applied these insights to the history of American political culture in a remarkable series of books that made plain his growing conservatism and his sense of alienation from what he called America's periodic "fits of moral crusading." *The Age of Reform* offered an interpretation of Populism and Progressivism "from the perspective of our own time." In his master's essay, Hofstadter had thoroughly sympathized with the struggles of the South's downtrodden tenant farmers. Now, he portrayed the

Populists of the late nineteenth century as small entrepreneurs standing against an inevitable tide of economic development. He saw them as taking refuge in a nostalgic agrarian myth or lashing out against imagined enemies from British bankers to Jews in a precursor to "modern authoritarian movements." (Interestingly, this interpretation still bore the mark of the traditional Marxist critique of petit-bourgeois social movements; the American Marxist thinker Daniel De Leon had said much the same thing in the 1890s.)

In *Social Darwinism*, William Graham Sumner and the capitalist plutocracy of the Gilded Age had emerged as the main threats to American democracy; while noting the underside of Progressivism—its racism and Anglo-Saxonism—Hofstadter seemed to embrace its demand for state activism against social injustice. In *The Age of Reform*, he depicted the Progressives as a displaced bourgeoisie seeking in political reform a way to overcome their decline in status. A similar sensibility informed Hofstadter's next two books. In *Anti-Intellectualism in American Life* (1963), he identified an American heartland "filled with people who are often fundamentalist in religion, nativist in prejudice, isolationist in foreign policy, and conservative in economics" as a persistent danger to intellectual life. In *The Paranoid Style in American Politics* (1965), he suggested that a common irrationality characterized popular enthusiasms of both the right and the left throughout American history.

The Age of Reform and *Anti-Intellectualism* won Hofstadter his two Pulitzer Prizes, but ironically, today both seem more dated than his earlier books. Their deep distrust of mass politics and their apparent dismissal of the substantive basis of reform movements strike the reader, even in today's conservative climate, as exaggerated and elitist. And since the rise of the new social history, it has become impossible to study mass movements without immersing oneself in local primary sources, rather than relying on the kind of imaginative reading of published works at which Hofstadter excelled. These books seemed to wed him to a consensus vision that deemed the American political system fundamentally sound and its critics essentially irrational.

Hofstadter's, however, was too protean an intellect to remain satisfied for long with the consensus framework. As social turmoil engulfed the country in the mid-1960s, he remained as prolific as ever, but his underlying assumptions shifted again. In *The Progressive Historians* (1968), he attempted to come to terms once and for all with Beard and his generation. Their portrait of an America racked by perennial conflict, he noted, was overdrawn, but by the same token, the consensus outlook could hardly explain the American Revolution, the Civil War or other key periods of turmoil in the nation's past (including, by implication, the 1960s). *American Violence* (1970), a documentary volume edited with his graduate student Michael Wallace, offered a chilling record of political and social turbulence that utterly contradicted the consensus vision of a nation placidly evolving without serious disagreements. Finally, in *America at 1750*, the first volume in a proposed three-part narrative history of the nation, Hofstadter offered a portrait that brilliantly took account of the paradoxical coexistence of individual freedom and opportunity and wide-spread social injustice and human bondage in the colonial era. The book remained unfinished at the time of his death from leukemia in 1971, offering only a tantalizing suggestion of what his full account of the American past might have been.

It was during the 1960s that I became acquainted with Richard Hofstadter, first as my adviser for an undergraduate senior thesis and later as supervisor of my doctoral dissertation. There was a certain irony in our relationship. Today, I am fortunate enough to occupy the DeWitt Clinton chair in history at Columbia, which Hofstadter once filled. Half a century ago, two years before I was born, the victim of political blacklisting Hofstadter replaced when he took his first full-time teaching position at City College was Jack Foner, my father.

Whatever thoughts Hofstadter harbored about this particular twist of fate, he played brilliantly the role of intellectual mentor so critical to any student's graduate career. For all his accomplishments he was utterly without pretension, always unintimidating, never too busy to talk about one's work. Hofstadter's books directed me toward the subjects that have defined my own writing—the history of political ideologies and the interconnections between social development and political culture. Not that he tried to impose his own interests or views on his students—far from it. If no "Hofstadter school" emerged from Columbia, it is because he had no desire to create one. Indeed, it often seemed during the 1960s that his graduate students, many of whom were actively involved in the civil rights and antiwar movements, were having as much influence on his evolving interests and outlook as he on theirs. (The idea for the book on American violence, for example, originated with Michael Wallace.)

Despite his death at the relatively young age of 54, Hofstadter left a prolific body of work, remarkable for its originality and readability, and for his capacity to range over the length and breadth of American history. From *Social Darwinism* to *America at 1750*, his writings stand as a model of what historical scholarship at its finest can aspire to achieve. ❖

Time for a Third Reconstruction

FEBRUARY 1, 1993

L ast month, the original copy of the Emancipation Proclamation was displayed at the National Archives. Issued on January 1, 1863, the proclamation sounded the death knell of slavery, thereby closing one chapter of American history and opening another, whose central issue was whether freedom for blacks implied genuine equality. Today, 130 years later, the task of bringing the descendants of slaves fully into the mainstream of American life remains to be accomplished.

It is unfortunate that Bill Clinton was out of Washington when the proclamation was exhibited. Had he perused the document and pondered its meaning, he might have been led to reflect on the First and Second Reconstructions—two moments, a century apart, when black and white Americans struggled to breathe substantive meaning into the freedom decreed during the Civil War. Their successes and failures suggest that the time has arrived for a Third Reconstruction, a renewed national effort to address the racial divide that afflicts our society.

The Emancipation Proclamation not only transformed the nature of the Civil War but opened the turbulent period of Reconstruction, in which the national government made its first effort to protect the equal rights of all Americans. Reconstruction is the most misunderstood era of our history. It was long viewed as a time of rampant corruption presided over by unscrupulous Northern carpetbaggers and former slaves unprepared for the freedom that had been thrust upon them. This interpretation helped to justify the subsequent policies of segregation and black disfranchisement in the South and the North's prolonged indifference to white Southerners' nullification of the federal Constitution.

In fact, Reconstruction was a laudable attempt to create, for the first time in our history, an interracial democracy. National civil rights laws and the Fourteenth and Fifteenth Amendments to the Constitution accorded the former slaves equality before the law and granted black men the right to vote.

Beginning in 1868, state and local governments resting on support from black voters and a minority of whites came to power throughout the South. They greatly expanded the states' social responsibilities, establishing public school systems, for example, where none had ever existed. These policies, and the spectacle of black men replacing the old slaveholding elite in offices from justice of the peace to US senator, provoked a campaign of violent opposition led by the Ku Klux Klan that, by 1877, had driven the last Reconstruction government from power.

Not until the civil rights movement of the 1950s and 1960s, often called the Second Reconstruction, did Americans again attempt to implement the unfulfilled social and political agenda of the post–Civil War years. In dismantling legal segregation, restoring to Southern blacks the right to vote and opening doors of economic and educational opportunity from which blacks had been almost entirely excluded, the Second Reconstruction achieved gains even more far-reaching than the first.

Nonetheless, we remain nearly as far from the ideal of a color-blind society as a century ago. As the First Reconstruction drew to a close, Thomas Wentworth Higginson, who had commanded a black regiment during the Civil War, commented, "Revolutions may go backward." Both Reconstructions were times of momentous hopes, followed by retrenchment, reaction and an attempt, sanctioned in the highest offices of the land, to undo much of what had been accomplished.

In both the late nineteenth century and the era of Reagan and Bush a century later, the federal government abandoned its commitment to the principle of equality and an active role in guaranteeing the rights of American citizens. Because it threatened traditions of local autonomy and was so closely associated with the new rights of blacks, the increased power of the federal government during the two Reconstructions generated powerful opposition. In both eras, opponents of equality raised the specter of a federal bureaucracy trampling on the rights of white citizens, warning that government efforts to combat the heritage of discrimination violated the immutable laws of the marketplace and made blacks privileged wards of the state. In both, social theories flourished that explained poverty as a consciously chosen way of life rather than a structural problem affecting the entire economy but for historical reasons most severe among the former slaves and their descendants.

The end of the First Reconstruction was a disaster for black Americans and profoundly affected the course of the nation's development. By 1900, Southern blacks were locked in a system of political, economic and social inequality, and the ideologies of social Darwinism and racism reigned supreme in both North and South. The exclusion of former slaves from the "political nation" left the Solid South under the control of a reactionary elite and shifted the spectrum of national politics significantly to the right.

The verdict is still out on the ultimate fate of the Second Reconstruction. But separate and unequal still rules in our schools, housing, job markets and conditions of life.

Indeed, both Reconstructions foundered, in large measure, because they failed to address the problem of economic equality. The first granted blacks equal rights before the law, but the government's refusal to redistribute land in the South left the freed people with no alternative but to compete as "free laborers" in a society in which all the economic cards were stacked against them. The second failed to confront effectively the economic gap separating black and white Americans.

The workings of the free market will not solve this problem, nor will a general policy of economic growth, whose benefits, history suggests, will not trickle down to the least fortunate. A Third Reconstruction is needed to address directly the economic inequalities that are the accumulated consequence of 250 years of slavery and a century of discrimination.

Today, of course, the nation's racial landscape is far more complex than in the nineteenth century. "Black and white" no longer adequately describes, if it ever did, the makeup of our society. The multiplicity of groups now claiming the status of victimized minority obscures the unique social and economic exploitation black Americans have suffered.

The black community itself is more divided than a century ago. An expanded middle class has arisen in the past generation, while social disintegration stalks the bottom of black society, spawning a pattern of violence that has fueled a right-wing backlash, making the task of addressing racial inequalities all the more difficult.

A national commitment to a Third Reconstruction would require the kind of moral leadership and political courage this generation is unaccustomed to in its presidents. But let us not forget that emancipation itself was not universally popular.

In 1864, some Republicans feared that a reaction against the destruction of slavery would cost their party the next election, and urged that the proclamation be rescinded. If he were to do so, Lincoln replied, "I should be damned in time and eternity." Can we hope for the same courage and sense of historical obligation from the incoming administration? ❖

Hiring Quotas for White Males Only

JUNE 26, 1995

Thirty-two years ago, I graduated from Columbia College. My class of 700 was all male and virtually all white. Most of us were young men of ability, yet had we been forced to compete for admission with women and racial minorities, fewer than half of us would have been at Columbia. None of us, to my knowledge, suffered debilitating self-doubt because we were the beneficiaries of affirmative action—that is, favored treatment on the basis of our race and gender.

Affirmative action has emerged as the latest "wedge issue" of American politics. The recent abrogation of California affirmative-action programs by Governor Pete Wilson, and the Clinton administration's halting efforts to re-evaluate federal policy, suggest the issue is coming to a head. As a historian, I find the current debate dismaying not only because of the crass effort to set Americans against one another for partisan advantage but also because the entire discussion lacks a sense of history.

Opponents of affirmative action, for example, have tried to wrap themselves in the mantle of the civil rights movement, seizing upon the 1963 speech in which Martin Luther King Jr. looked forward to the time when his children would be judged not by the "color of their skin" but by the "content of their character." Rarely mentioned is that King came to be a strong supporter of affirmative action.

In his last book, *Where Do We Go From Here?*, a brooding meditation on America's long history of racism, King acknowledged that "special treatment" for blacks seemed to conflict with the ideal of opportunity based on individual merit. But, he continued, "a society that has done something special *against* the Negro for hundreds of years must now do something special *for* him."

Our country, King realized, has never operated on a color-blind basis. From the beginning of the Republic, membership in American society was defined in racial terms. The first naturalization law, enacted in 1790, restricted citizenship for those emigrating from abroad to "free white persons." Free blacks, even in the North, were barred from juries, public schools, government employment and the militia and regular army. Not until after the Civil War were blacks deemed worthy to be American citizens, while Asians were barred from naturalization until the 1940s.

White immigrants certainly faced discrimination. But they had access to the political power, jobs and residential neighborhoods denied to blacks. In the nineteenth century, the men among them enjoyed the right to vote even before they were naturalized. Until well into this century, however, the vast majority of black Americans were excluded from the suffrage except for a period immediately after the Civil War. White men, native and immigrant, could find well-paid craft and industrial jobs, while employers and unions limited nonwhites (and women) to unskilled and menial employment. The "American standard of living" was an entitlement of white men alone.

There is no point in dwelling morbidly on past injustices. But this record of unequal treatment cannot be dismissed as "vague or ancient wrongs" with no bearing on the present, as Republican strategist William Kristol recently claimed. Slavery may be gone and legal segregation dismantled, but the effects of past discrimination live on in seniority systems that preserve intact the results of a racially segmented job market, a black unemployment rate double that of whites and pervasive housing segregation.

Past racism is embedded in the two-tier, racially divided system of social insurance still on the books today. Because key congressional committees in the 1930s were controlled by Southerners with all-white electorates, they did not allow the supposedly universal entitlement of Social Security to cover the largest categories of black workers—agricultural laborers and domestics. Social Security excluded 80 percent of employed black women, who were forced to depend for a safety net on the much less generous "welfare" system.

The notion that affirmative action stigmatizes its recipients reflects not just belief in advancement according to individual merit but the older idea that the "normal" American is white. There are firemen and black firemen, construction workers and black construction workers: Nonwhites (and women) who obtain such jobs are still widely viewed as interlopers, depriving white men of positions or promotions to which they are historically entitled.

I have yet to meet the white male in whom special favoritism (getting a job, for example, through relatives or an old boys' network, or because of racial discrimination by a union or employer) fostered doubt about his own abilities. In a society where belief in black inferiority is still widespread (witness the success of *The Bell Curve*), many whites and some blacks may question the abilities of beneficiaries of affirmative action. But this social "cost" hardly counterbalances the enormous social benefits affirmative action has produced.

Nonwhites (and even more so, white women) have made deep inroads into the lower middle class and into professions once reserved for white males. Columbia College now admits women and minority students. Would these and other opportunities have opened as widely and as quickly without the pressure of affirmative-action programs? American history suggests they would not.

It is certainly true, as critics charge, that affirmative action's benefits have not spread to the poorest members of the black community. The children of Harlem, regrettably, are not in a position to take advantage of the spots Columbia has opened to blacks. But rather than simply ratifying the advantages of already affluent blacks, who traditionally advanced by servicing the seg-regated black community, affirmative action has helped to create a new black middle class, resting on professional and managerial positions within white society.

This new class is much more vulnerable than its white counterpart to the shifting fortunes of the economy and politics. Far more middle-class blacks than whites depend on public employment —positions now threatened by the downsizing of federal, state and municipal governments. The fact that other actions are needed to address the problems of the "underclass" hardly negates the proven value of affirmative action in expanding black access to the middle class and skilled working class.

There is no harm in rethinking the ways affirmative action is implemented—re-examining, for example, the expansion to numerous other groups of a program originally intended to deal with the legacy of slavery and segregation. In principle, there may well be merit in redefining disadvantage to include poor whites. The present cry for affirmative action based on class rather than race, however, seems as much an evasion as a serious effort to rethink public policy. Efforts to uplift the poor, while indispensable in a just society, are neither a substitute for nor incompatible with programs that address the legacy of the race-based discrimination to which blacks have historically been subjected. Without a robust class politics, moreover, class policies are unlikely to get very far. The present Congress may well dismantle affirmative action, but it hardly seems sympathetic to broad "color-blind" programs to assist the poor.

At a time of deindustrialization and stagnant real wages, many whites have come to blame affirmative action for declining economic prospects. Let us not delude ourselves, however, into thinking that eliminating affirmative action will produce a society in which rewards are based on merit. Despite our rhetoric, equal opportunity has never been the American way. For nearly all our history, affirmative action has been a prerogative of white men. ❖

The Great Divide

OCTOBER 30, 1995

D espite the rapid growth of Asian and Hispanic populations that renders this country's familiar bipolar racial paradigm increasingly obsolete, the black-white divide remains the most intractable fissure in American life. The acquittal of O.J. Simpson has underscored, once again, the chasm that separates black and white Americans. With nationalist sentiment on the rise in the black community, a conservative politics indifferent to racial inequality ascendant among whites and many on the left entranced by their own group causes, the ideal of an integrated society seems more remote than ever. In the face of these realities, is it possible to reassert the validity and vitality of a politics of integration?

I believe it is not only possible but necessary. First, however, we must candidly assess what has and has not changed in the three decades since the Kerner Commission concluded that the United States consisted of two societies, black and white, separate and unequal. Today legal segregation is dead, blacks vote in the same proportion as whites, and many realms of life—sports, politics, entertainment, higher education and certain echelons of middle-class employment—are far more integrated than was conceivable at the dawn of the civil rights era. On the other hand, not only have the black working class and poor fallen further behind their white counterparts but the crucial, interrelated areas of housing and schools remain predominantly segregated, if not by law then by custom buttressed by economics and public policy.

To reaffirm a politics of integration it is necessary to confront the uncomfortable truth that, contrary to fashionable punditry, there never was a golden age of racial harmony, a liberal consensus destroyed by black nationalists and white multiculturalists. America's residential apartheid results from a long history of government policy, individual choices and the inequitable operation of a putatively free market. Well before the turn from civil rights to black power or the rise of crime rates, illegitimacy and drug use in poor black communities, the federal government institutionalized racial segregation in New Deal public housing and mortgage policies, and private developers systematically excluded blacks from the postwar suburban boom. The September issue of the *Journal of American History* contains revealing and disturbing articles about the prolonged, violent opposition in postwar Chicago and Detroit to even the smallest black presence in white neighborhoods. The residents' fear was not crime or drugs but a decline in property values and black competition for jobs traditionally reserved for whites.

Then as now, whiteness had an economic value. It soon revealed its political potency as well. Even at the height of the

1960s, for example, it was a successful referendum campaign to rescind a fair housing law that galvanized California's grassroots conservatism.

The point is not to paint all whites with the brush of unyielding racism. Such a generalization would be as unfair as current conservative dogma that blacks are immersed in a culture of drugs and illegitimacy. Throughout our history, from the abolitionists to the civil rights era, countless whites have fought for a society in which all citizens enjoyed equal rights and equal opportunities.

It is too often forgotten that integration is a very radical idea, not a stuffy nostrum, as critics of the NAACP have long claimed. In fact, our society can far more easily accommodate a program of separatism, group identity and autonomy for local black institutions—whether emanating from the Garvey movement, black power advocates or the Million Man March—than a program of genuine integration.

From Frederick Douglass and Wendell Phillips in the nineteenth century to Martin Luther King Jr., integration has meant not the absorption of blacks into the pre-existing white social order but the *transformation* of American society so as to give real meaning to the principle of equality. Properly understood, integration means not only the removal of economic, social and political obstacles to full participation in every area of American life but changes in the contours of personal life so that friendship, comradeship and intimacy between the races can become far more common than is possible today. To our cynical age, this sentiment may seem rather mawkish, just as the old abolitionist maxim about the slave—Am I Not a Man and a Brother?—appears to many naïve or paternalistic. But ultimately, a belief in brotherhood lies at the heart of any politics of integration.

At a time when many blacks express an understandable despair for the future and nostalgia for segregation, with its strong black-run institutions, and when many whites seem content to retreat into private schools and gated communities, the idea of integration seems more utopian than ever, requiring not only the passage of new laws but a change in Americans' hearts and minds. Since the days of the abolitionists, however, the role of the left has been to put forward utopian ideas, to offer a moral and political critique of existing institutions, to worry less about what is politically possible than about what might be. The time has come to reintroduce integration into our political vocabulary—not as a code for whites dictating to blacks or as "color-blindness," a term appropriated from the civil rights movement by conservatives and made into an empty slogan, but as a vision of a nation transformed, one in which equality is a reality for all Americans. ❖

Our Monumental Mistakes

NOVEMBER 8, 1999

Review of *Lies Across America: What Our Historic Sites Get Wrong*, by James W. Loewen

To the surprise of historians themselves, history—or at least its public presentation—has become big business. The Freedom Trail, a walking tour of monuments, buildings and historical markers, is Boston's leading tourist attraction. The History Channel is among the most successful enterprises on cable television, and attendance at historical museums and other sites is at a record high.

What account of the past does our public history convey? This is the question James Loewen sets out to answer. A former professor at the University of Vermont, Loewen is a one-man historical truth squad, best known as the author of *Lies My Teacher Told Me*, which argued that high school history texts are laced with misconceptions, omissions and outright lies. In *Lies Across America*, based on visits to historic markers, houses and monuments in all fifty states, Loewen comes to essentially the same conclusion about the public presentation of American history.

Friedrich Nietzsche once identified three approaches to history: monumental, antiquarian and critical (the last defined as "the history that judges and condemns"). Nearly all historical monuments, of course, are meant to be flattering to their subjects; it is probably asking too much to expect them to be critical in Nietzsche's sense. But one can expect basic accuracy and honesty, and this test, as Loewen demonstrates, much of our public history fails.

Problems begin with the language commonly used to describe early American history, which suggests that the continent was uninhabited before white settlement and that only people of English origin qualify as "civilized." Now excised from most historians' accounts of Columbus's voyages, the much-abused word "discovery" remains alive and well on historical markers, even where self-evidently inappropriate. A marker in Iowa declares that the French explorer Jean Nicolet "discovered" Okamanpadu Lake, although Indians had clearly named it well before Nicolet's arrival. A Minnesota marker credits Henry Schoolcraft with the "discovery" of Lake Itasca, the source of the Mississippi River, even while acknowledging that the lake was "known to Indians and traders" well before Schoolcraft's arrival in 1832. In Gardner, Kansas, where the Oregon and Santa Fe trails diverge, a marker honors the "pioneers who brought civilization to the western half of the United States"—thus expelling from history not only Indian populations but the Spanish, who planted their civilizations in the West centuries before the advent of overland settlers.

But what really concerns Loewen is not so much misrepresentations such as these but lies of omission. Nietzsche spoke of "creative forgetfulness" as essential to historical memory; what is not memorialized tells us as much about a society's sense of the past as what is. For Loewen, the great scandal of our public history is the treatment of slavery, the Civil War and the country's long history of racial injustice.

Amnesia best describes America's official stance regarding slavery. Visitors to Washington, DC, will find a national museum devoted to the Holocaust, funded annually with millions of taxpayer dollars, but almost nothing related to slavery, our home-grown crime against humanity. Tours of historic plantations, Loewen notes, ignore or sugarcoat the lives of slaves. No whips, chains or other artifacts of discipline are on display, and presentations by guides focus on the furniture, gardens and architecture rather than the role of slave labor in creating the wealth they represent.

At Hannibal, Missouri, whose principal industry is the commemoration of native son Mark Twain, the fact that Twain grew up in a slave society remains unmentioned, and a two-hour outdoor pageant based on *Huckleberry Finn* manages to eliminate Jim, the runaway slave on whose plight the book pivots. The slave trade, a central element of the pre–Civil War Southern economy, has also disappeared from public history. In Alexandria, Virginia, the Franklin and Armfield Office bears a plaque designating it as a National Historic Landmark. That this elegant building served as headquarters for the city's largest slave dealer is conveniently forgotten.

Especially but not exclusively in the South, Civil War monuments glorify soldiers and generals who fought for Southern independence, explaining their motivation by reference to the ideals of freedom, states' rights and individual autonomy—everything, that is, but slavery, the "cornerstone of the Confederacy," according to its vice president, Alexander Stephens. Fort Mill, South Carolina, has a marker honoring the "faithful slaves" of the Confederate states, but one would be hard pressed to find monuments anywhere in the country to slave rebels like Denmark Vesey and Nat Turner, to the 200,000 black soldiers and sailors who fought for the Union (or, for that matter, the thousands of white Southerners who remained loyal to the nation). Even at Gettysburg, the most frequently visited Civil War historic park and site of the Union's most celebrated military victory, the emotional focus of the presentation is the sacrifice of gallant Southern soldiers in Pickett's charge. No gallantry seems to attach to those who fought for the Union.

* * *

As Loewen points out, most Confederate monuments were erected between 1890 and 1920 under the leadership of the United Daughters of the Confederacy as part of a conscious effort to glorify and sanitize the Confederate cause and legitimize the newly installed Jim Crow system. Gen. Nathan Bedford Forrest, "one of the most vicious racists in U.S. history," as Loewen puts it, was a slave trader, founder of the Ku Klux Klan and commander of troops who massacred black Union soldiers after their surrender at Fort Pillow. Yet there are more statues, markers and busts of Forrest in Tennessee than of any other figure in the state's history, including President Andrew Jackson. Only one transgression was sufficiently outrageous to disqualify Confederate leaders from the pantheon of heroes. No statue of James Longstreet, a far abler commander than Forrest, graces the Southern countryside, and Gen. James Fleming is omitted from the portrait gallery of famous figures of Arkansas history in Little Rock. Their crime? Both supported black rights during Reconstruction.

Even today, Loewen points out, Reconstruction, the period after the Civil War when interracial democracy briefly flourished in the South, is almost invisible in America's public history. Guides at plantations rarely mention what happened after emancipation, and there are no statues of Reconstruction governors or of the era's numerous black political leaders. Meanwhile, a monument to the White League of Louisiana, a terrorist organization that led a violent uprising in 1874 to restore white supremacy, still stands in New Orleans, although there was recent controversy over its possible removal.

The same pattern of evasion and misrepresentation marks post-Reconstruction racial history. Texas has nearly 12,000 historical markers—more than the rest of the country combined—but not one mentions any of the state's numerous lynchings, the Brownsville race riot of 1906 or even *Sweatt v. Painter*, the landmark civil rights case that paved the way for the *Brown* school-desegregation decision. Downtown Scottsboro, Alabama, contains four historical markers, but none touch on the only event for which the town is famous: the 1930s trials in which nine young black men were wrongly convicted of rape. A trio of markers in Louisiana celebrate the life of Leander Perez for his "dedicated service to the people of Plaquemines Parish," without mentioning that he referred to Plaquemines's blacks as "animals right out of the jungle" and fought a bitter battle against racial integration. Such forgetfulness is not confined to the South. The plaque on the statue of Orville Hubbard, mayor of Dearborn, Michigan, from 1942 to 1978, praises his achievements in snow removal and trash collection but fails to take note of his outspoken and successful efforts to keep the city lily white (when he left office, fewer than twenty of Dearborn's 90,000 inhabitants were black).

* * *

Slavery and its legacy are not the only aspects of our history to be sanitized, romanticized or ignored in what Loewen calls our historical "landscape of denial." American radicalism is generally excised from public history. Helen Keller's birthplace in Tuscumbia, Alabama, contains no mention of her support for labor unions, socialism or black rights. A marker at Finn Hall in southwestern Washington notes the weddings, athletic competitions and other events held there by Finnish immigrants without acknowledging their socialist convictions or that the association that constructed the building called itself the "Comrades Society."

Commemorations of wars are also highly selective. Numerous plaques and statues honor those who served in the Spanish-American War; none, however, tell the story of America's brutal suppression of the Philippine movement for independence that followed. Despite the popularity of the Vietnam Memorial in Washington, DC,

America's longest war remains too controversial to mention elsewhere. The aircraft carrier USS *Intrepid*, now anchored at a Manhattan pier as a floating war memorial, saw extended duty in World War II and Vietnam. But the onboard historical presentation deals only with the ship's role in the first of these conflicts, despite complaints from Vietnam veterans about being written out of history.

Overall, Loewen has written a devastating portrait of how American history is commemorated. The book is lively and informative, and his mini-essays correcting the errors and omissions at various sites offer valuable history lessons in themselves. Loewen does take note of recent efforts to diversify and modernize public history. Montana has introduced new markers on aspects of Indian history, and Pennsylvania recently decided to commemorate the state's African-American past. But perhaps because he is so intent on exposing the deficiencies of the historical landscape, Loewen fails to give adequate attention to larger debates and changes now under way.

* * *

Loewen does not analyze the visiting experience itself, or the possibility that people attuned to newer perspectives on the past may come away from monuments and exhibits with rather different impressions than their originators intended, or may contest how history is being presented. He offers no account, for example, of the controversy over history at the Alamo, where Mexican-Americans and others are challenging the representation of the fort's white defenders as champions of liberty while ignoring the expropriation of Mexican lands and the expansion of slavery that were an essential part of the movement for Texas independence. He notes that Boston's Freedom Trail has been supplemented by a Women's Heritage Trail, a Black Heritage Trail and even a guide to the city's gay and lesbian history, but fails to reflect on how the quest for tourist dollars can be a spur to diversifying public history.

Loewen says nothing about the efforts of the National Park Service, under chief historian Dwight Pitcaithley, to re-evaluate the hundreds of sites under its control. Slavery may be ignored in most public presentations of history, but the Park Service is currently developing a historical site in Natchez, Mississippi, devoted to the experiences of slaves and free blacks in the city's history. Gettysburg still offers a neo-Confederate view of the Civil War, but the park's directors have developed an ambitious plan to place military events there in the context of the era's social and political history, including the history of slavery.

These developments, while salutary, do not negate the overall force of Loewen's critique. Why, one wonders, has our understanding of history changed so rapidly, but its public presentation remained so static? Ultimately, public monuments are built by those with sufficient power to determine which parts of history are worth commemorating and what vision of history ought to be conveyed. One of Loewen's more interesting observations is that while labor history is almost entirely ignored in textbooks, it enjoys considerable presence in public monuments. Because unions possess economic power and political influence, they have been able to persuade states to erect markers commemorating strikes and confrontations between labor and the police, as well as noting mine and factory disasters.

Nonetheless, powerful forces remain resistant to change—a lesson the Smithsonian Institution learned a few years ago when protests from veterans' organizations scuttled a proposed exhibit on the dropping of the first atomic bomb because it pointed out that military officials disagreed over the necessity for the weapon's use. Regarding the racism so powerfully embedded in our public history, what is surprising is not that monuments and markers erected a century ago reflect the views of the Jim Crow era but that many Americans remain wedded to these representations.

Americans applauded the Muscovites who in 1991 toppled the statue of Felix Dzerzhinsky, founder of the Soviet secret police, but citizens of New Orleans who demanded the removal of the monument glorifying the White League were denounced as "Stalinists" by a leading historian in the pages of the *New York Times*. The point is not that every monument to a slaveholder ought to be dismantled but that existing historical sites must be revised to convey a more complex and honest view of our past, and that statues of black Civil War soldiers, slave rebels, civil rights activists and the like should share public space with Confederate generals and Klansmen, all of them part of America's history. ❖

Rebel Yell

The recent march in Columbia, South Carolina, demanding the removal of the Confederate battle flag from atop the state capitol is the latest episode in a long-running debate over the legacy of slavery and the Civil War. Those who seek to retain the flag have lately sought to reposition the Old South and the Confederacy in American memory. The Confederate flag, they tell us, represents not slavery but local identity, a way of life and respect for "heritage." Some defenders of the flag go so far as to paint the pre–Civil War South as a multicultural paradise where black and white lived in harmony, and they claim that legions of slaves enlisted to fight for the Confederate cause.

There is no better way to honor one's forebears than by taking their ideas seriously. To understand what the flag now flying in Columbia represents, one need only read the Declaration of the Immediate Causes of Secession, adopted by the South Carolina secession convention in December 1860. Modeled on the Declaration of Independence of 1776, it marshaled arguments that the authors hoped would inspire the rest of the South to secede.

South Carolina's statesmen identified the preservation of slavery as their overriding concern. States' rights and regional loyalty, often cited today as the real meaning of the Confederate flag, were invoked only as these doctrines protected slavery. The North, the declaration insisted, had "assumed the right of deciding on the propriety of our domestic institutions." Abraham Lincoln, recently elected president, was a man "whose opinions and purposes are hostile to slavery" and under whose administration the institution would not be safe. "There can be but one end by the submission of the South to the rule of a sectional antislavery government at Washington," the Declaration concluded: "the emancipation of the slaves of the South."

Slavery, as Southern Vice President Alexander Stephens put it, was "the cornerstone" of the Confederacy. This does not mean that it was the only issue contributing to the coming of the Civil War. Nor does it suggest that the hundreds of thousands of men who fought under the Confederate banner, most of them non-slaveholders, were motivated exclusively by the desire to keep blacks in bondage. Yet to claim that Confederate soldiers went to war to protect their "way of life" conveniently forgets that this way of life was founded on slavery.

Slaves fully understood this. A few light-skinned blacks may have passed for white and joined the Southern Army. But the regiments of black Confederate troops one hears about of late exist only in myth or in the willful confusion of the Army's black servants and laborers—slaves impressed into service by their masters—with combat soldiers. The reality is that hundreds of thousands of slaves eagerly sought their freedom by fleeing to Union lines and enlisting in the Union Army.

Despite claims that the flying of the Confederate flag is a tradition dating back to the Civil War, the fact is that for years after that devastating conflict few white Southerners felt any desire to memorialize the Confederacy. The cult of the Lost Cause did not flourish until the 1890s, just as a new system of racial inequality resting on disenfranchisement and segregation was being created throughout the South.

Not until a century after the Civil War did South Carolina's white leaders feel the need to display the flag above the Capitol, for reasons that had more to do with the 1960s than the 1860s. In March 1961, as the Civil War centennial celebration began in Charleston, a black member of the New Jersey delegation was denied admission to the headquarters hotel. President Kennedy then transferred the meeting to a nearby naval base, whereupon the South Carolina delegation seceded, holding its own "Confederate States Centennial Conference," with the Confederate flag prominently displayed. A year later, the flag was mounted above the state capitol as a gesture of defiance against the civil rights movement. To the flag's previous association with slavery was now added a connotation of racial segregation.

Public monuments, historical markers and symbols reflect what a society thinks should be commemorated. One hopes that when the Confederate flag comes down, as now seems inevitable, the myths that prevent a full acknowledgment of the central place of slavery and racial injustice in our nation's history will also be laid to rest. ❖

Shedding Lincoln's Mantle

AUGUST 7, 2000

American politicians are not noted for their histori-cal self-consciousness. But the Republican delegates now gathering in Philadelphia would do well to devote some thought to their party's history. The first Republican nominating convention, in 1856, also took place in the City of Brotherly Love. But that party was a far different institution from its counterpart today.

A coalition of Democrats, Whigs and abolitionists who had united to oppose the expansion of slavery, the Republican Party was defeated in 1856 but four years later elected Abraham Lincoln to the White House. "Free labor" was the new party's rallying cry, by which Republicans meant labor unshackled by slavery or aristocratic privilege and able to achieve economic independence through owning a small farm or artisan shop. The opportunities enjoyed by ordinary workers, Republicans insisted, distinguished the "free society" of the North from the slave South.

There were blind spots in the party's outlook, most notably concerning Catholic immigrants. In the 1850s and for many years thereafter, part of the Republican base lay among nativists hostile to immigration. But into the twentieth century, most advocates of social change, including blacks, feminists and Progressive-era reformers, moved in the party's orbit.

The early Republican Party was a strictly Northern institution. It established a Southern presence only in the wake of Union victory in the Civil War. That war and the Reconstruction era that followed witnessed the party's greatest accomplishments: emancipation of the slaves, passage of the first national civil rights legislation, adoption of the Fourteenth Amendment—which became the main constitutional safeguard of individual rights—and granting black men the right to vote in an effort to create a functioning interracial democracy in the South. The war that destroyed slavery elevated equality before the law for all Americans, secured by a newly empowered national government, to a central place in Republican ideology.

Over time, as Republican leaders increasingly came under the sway of Northern railroad men and industrialists, the Republican Party would abandon its commitment to the rights of African-Americans, acquiescing in the overthrow of Reconstruction and the imposition of segregation. When the South disenfranchised its black voters around the turn of the century, Republicans once again found themselves a Northern party, while the South remained solidly Democratic for more than half a century. As Republicans became more and more associated with the interests of Northern business, free labor metamorphosed into "freedom of contract"—the belief that what defined a worker's liberty was the ability to sell one's labor in the economic marketplace without interference or regulation by government.

Today's Republicans are far different from their forebears. The party of free labor is deeply hostile to unions and devoted to corporate interests. The party that secured the Union and viewed the federal government, in the words of Massachusetts Senator Charles Sumner, as "the custodian of freedom," has adopted the Old South's belief in state sovereignty. The party on which generations of feminists pinned their hopes now harbors the most virulent opponents of a woman's right to control her own person. The party that in its 1856 platform condemned as international brigandage the Ostend Manifesto, which called for the United States to "wrest" Cuba from Spain, now appears to view Cuba as by rights a wholly owned subsidiary of the United States.

Most striking, the party of emancipation and Reconstruction has become deeply hostile to civil rights enforcement, affirmative action—indeed, any measures that seek to redress the enduring consequences of slavery and segregation. Republicans, George W. Bush acknowledged in his recent speech before the NAACP, have "not always carried the mantle of Lincoln." This was quite an understatement. Ever since Barry Goldwater carried five states of the Deep South, proving that Republicans could rebuild their Southern wing by appealing to white resentment over civil rights gains, Republicans have adhered to a Southern strategy that has turned most of the levers of power within the party over to the white South and the conservative extended South, which stretches into the Southwest and Southern California.

In 1996 Republicans even advocated the repeal of one of the party's crowning achievements, the section of the Fourteenth Amendment that bestows citizenship on all persons born in the United States. Their platform called for denying citizenship to the children of people who entered the United States illegally or "are not long-term residents." At this writing it is not clear whether this example of uncompassionate conservatism will be retained in this year's platform. Here Republicans were true to their history or at least to its nativist element. Unfortunately, today's Republicans have abandoned the best parts of their heritage while retaining the worst. ✤

Partisanship Rules

JANUARY 1, 2001

The Supreme Court decision effectively handing the presidency to George W. Bush reveals the intensely partisan nature of the court's current majority. The court, to be sure, has always been political, but rarely as blatantly as today. Nor are there many precedents for justices trampling on their own previous convictions to reach a predetermined conclusion.

Chief Justice Roger Taney enlisted the aid of President-elect James Buchanan in persuading Northern Justices to join the pro-slavery majority in *Dred Scott*. Franklin Roosevelt conferred regularly with Justice Louis Brandeis, and Justice Abe Fortas served as a trusted political adviser of Lyndon Johnson. But never has there been a public statement as partisan as Antonin Scalia's when first suspending the recounts that the court needed to insure "public acceptance" of a Bush presidency.

If there is a silver lining, it is that the last month suggests an agenda for democratic reform. First, the electoral college should be abolished. The product of an entirely different political era,

when the electorate excluded women, nonwhites and proper-
tyless males, the electoral college was created by a generation
fearful of democracy. Its aim was to place the choice of president
in the hands of each state's most prominent men, not the voters.
It unfairly enhances the power of the least populous states and
can produce the current spectacle of a candidate receiving a
majority of the votes but losing the election. At the very least,
electors should be chosen in proportion to the popular vote in
each state.

Second, the Florida fiasco should lead to the reform of voting
procedures. As with schools, roads and public services, the wealth-
iest districts have the best system of voting. The machines used in
poor black precincts of Florida, the *Miami Herald* demonstrated,
are so flawed that they are guaranteed to produce a larger number
of spoiled or uncounted ballots than in affluent suburban areas.

One can only view with deep cynicism the court majority's
invocation of "equal protection" in rejecting a recount. Added to
the Constitution in the Fourteenth Amendment after the Civil
War, this language was intended to protect former slaves from
discriminatory state actions and to establish the principle that
citizens' rights are uniform throughout the nation. The current
court's concept of equal protection has essentially boiled down
to supporting white plaintiffs who claim to be disadvantaged by
affirmative action.

Nonetheless, by extending the issue of equal protection to
the casting and counting of votes, the court has opened the door
to challenging our highly inequitable system of voting. Claims of

unequal treatment by voters in poorer districts are not likely to receive a sympathetic hearing from the current majority. But *Bush v. Gore* may galvanize demands for genuine equality of participation in the democratic process that legislatures and a future court may view sympathetically.

Equally difficult to accept at face value is the majority's disdain for the principle of federalism these very justices have trumpeted for the past several years. Like the South before the Civil War, which believed in states' rights but demanded a fugitive-slave law that overrode the North's judicial and police machinery, today's majority seems to view constitutional principles as remarkably malleable when powerful interests are at stake.

The next time this court turns down an appeal by a death-row inmate on the grounds that federalism requires it to respect local judicial procedures, the condemned plaintiff may well wonder why his claims do not merit the same consideration as those of the Republican candidate for president. ❖

Southern Comfort

nce again, the Civil War has sparked a contemporary political controversy. Two of President Bush's cabinet nominees—Attorney General-designate John Ashcroft and the prospective Secretary of the Interior, Gale Norton—are being asked to explain their praise of the Confederacy.

In a 1996 speech to a conservative group, Norton likened her struggle to preserve states' rights to the Confederate rebellion, saying, "We lost too much" when the Union triumphed. Ashcroft, in a 1998 interview, lauded the magazine *Southern Partisan* for defending "patriots" like Robert E. Lee and Jefferson Davis and called on "traditionalists" to vindicate the Confederate cause against charges that it represented a "perverted agenda."

What is it about the Confederacy that appeals to so many modern-day conservatives from the party of Lincoln? Neither Ashcroft nor Norton appears to have family roots below the Mason-Dixon line. Ashcroft was born in Chicago, raised in Missouri and educated at Yale. Norton grew up in Colorado.

But what is interesting is how conservatives who feel themselves heritage-deficient gravitate to a romanticized memory of the Old South—a usable past that conveniently omits slavery and Jim Crow.

During the 1950s, many conservatives responded favorably to Southern white resistance to desegregation. Moral conservatives saw the white South as a last bastion of traditional Christian civilization in a nation pervaded by individualism and secularism. Many libertarians insisted that federal action to secure civil rights threatened local autonomy, displaying an amazing indifference to the historic denial of blacks' rights by state and local authorities. Then in 1964, Barry Goldwater, who opposed that year's Civil Rights Act, carried five Deep South states, demonstrating that Republicans could strike electoral gold by appealing to white voters' resentment over black gains. Since then, white Southerners have become the backbone of the party's electoral strength.

Over the past two decades, *Southern Partisan* has carried articles defending apartheid, denying that slavery is contrary to Christian values, calling Lincoln a greater tyrant than George III, insisting that "Negroes, Asians, and Orientals ... Hispanics, Latins, and Eastern Europeans have no temperament for democracy" and lamenting that immigration is undermining the "genetic racial pool" of the United States. Yet Ashcroft is hardly the only conservative to identify with the magazine. The advisers and contributing editors listed on its masthead have included Russell Kirk, a founding father of modern conservatism, and Republican politicians like Pat Buchanan and North Carolina Congressman David Funderburk.

Most Republicans appeal more subtly to white Southern voters. Ronald Reagan opened his 1984 campaign in Philadelphia, Mississippi, where three civil rights workers were slain; George W. Bush sent a message by speaking at Bob Jones University. Lauding the Confederacy is part of this symbolic politics.

No one claims that Ashcroft or Norton wants to restore slavery. But at the very least, their statements reflect a remarkable tone-deafness to how praise of the Confederacy is likely to be received outside conservative ranks. They tell us something about the restricted boundaries of the world of modern conservatism.

When it comes to the Civil War, Bush's cabinet is a house divided. Ashcroft and Norton could benefit from a conversation—perhaps on Lincoln's Birthday—with Secretary of State Colin Powell. To Ashcroft and Norton, the South equals the white South, which equals the Confederacy. Blacks are not real Southerners, the region's white Unionists did not exist and slavery—the "cornerstone" of the Confederacy according to its vice president, Alexander Stephens—had nothing to do with the Civil War. Norton describes slavery as a "bad fact," legal parlance for an irrelevancy that inconveniently muddies the judicial waters, like smog on a day when a corporate polluter is defending itself in court.

Powell, on the other hand, has lectured eloquently about the contribution of black soldiers (nearly all of them Southern-born) to Union victory and the centrality of emancipation to that era's history. He could teach his colleagues something about the complexity of Southern history and the real meaning of the Civil War. Not that he is likely to be asked by the members of Bush's new cabinet. ✤

The Most Patriotic Act

OCTOBER 8, 2001

The drumbeat now begins, as it always does in time of war: We must accept limitations on our liberties. The FBI and CIA should be "unleashed" in the name of national security. Patriotism means uncritical support of whatever actions the president deems appropriate. Arab-Americans, followers of Islam, people with Middle Eastern names or ancestors, should be subject to special scrutiny by the government and their fellow citizens. With liberal members of congress silent and the administration promising a war on terrorism lasting "years, not days," such sentiments are likely to be with us for some time to come.

Of the many lessons of American history, this is among the most basic. Our civil rights and civil liberties—freedom of expression, the right to criticize the government, equality before the law, restraints on the exercise of police powers—are not gifts from the state that can be rescinded when it desires. They are the inheritance of a long history of struggles: by abolitionists for the ability to hold meetings and publish their views in the face of mob violence; by labor leaders for the power to organize unions, picket and distribute literature without fear of arrest; by feminists for the right to disseminate birth-control information without being charged with violating the obscenity laws; and by all those who braved jail and worse to challenge entrenched systems of racial inequality.

The history of freedom in this country is not, as is often thought, the logical working out of ideas immanent in our founding documents or a straight-line trajectory of continual progress. It is a story of countless disagreements and battles in which victories sometimes prove temporary and retrogression often follows progress.

When critics of the original Constitution complained about the absence of a Bill of Rights, the Constitution's "father," James Madison, replied that no list of liberties could ever anticipate the ways government might act in the future. "Parchment barriers" to the abuse of authority, he wrote, would be least effective when most needed. Thankfully, the Bill of Rights was eventually adopted. But Madison's observation was amply borne out at moments of popular hysteria when freedom of expression was trampled in the name of patriotism and national unity.

Americans have notoriously short historical memories. But it is worth recalling some of those moments to understand how liberty has been endangered in the past. During the "quasiwar" with France in 1798, the Alien and Sedition Acts allowed deportation of immigrants deemed dangerous by federal authorities and made it illegal to criticize the federal government. During the Civil War, both sides jailed critics and suppressed opposition newspapers.

In World War I, German-Americans, socialists, labor leaders and critics of US involvement were subjected to severe government repression and assault by private vigilante groups. Publications critical of the war were banned from the mails, individuals were jailed for antiwar statements and in the Red Scare that followed the war thousands of radicals were arrested and numerous aliens deported. During World War II, tens of thousands of Japanese-Americans, most of them US citizens, were removed to internment camps. Sanctioned by the Supreme Court, this was the greatest violation of Americans' civil liberties, apart from slavery, in our history.

No one objects to more stringent security at airports. But current restrictions on the FBI and CIA limiting surveillance, wiretapping, infiltration of political groups at home and assassinations abroad do not arise from an irrational desire for liberty at the expense of security. They are the response to real abuses of authority, which should not be forgotten in the zeal to sweep them aside as "handcuffs" on law enforcement.

Before unleashing these agencies, let us recall the FBI's persistent harassment of citizens like Martin Luther King Jr. and its efforts to disrupt the civil rights and antiwar movements, and the CIA's history of cooperation with some of the world's most egregious violators of human rights. The principle that no group of Americans should be stigmatized as disloyal or criminal because of race or national origin is too recent and too fragile an achievement to be abandoned now.

Every war in American history, from the Revolution to the Gulf War, with the exception of World War II, inspired vigorous internal dissent. Self-imposed silence is as debilitating to a democracy as censorship. If questioning an ill-defined, open-ended "war on terrorism" is to be deemed unpatriotic, the same label will have to be applied to Abraham Lincoln at the time of the Mexican War, Jane Addams and Eugene V. Debs during World War I, and Wayne Morse and Ernest Gruening, who had the courage and foresight to vote against the Gulf of Tonkin resolution in 1964.

All of us today share a feeling of grief and outrage over the events of September 11 and a desire that those responsible for mass murder be brought to justice. But at times of crisis the most patriotic act of all is the unyielding defense of civil liberties, the right to dissent and equality before the law for all Americans. ❖

Changing History

SEPTEMBER 23, 2002

This was a contribution to The Nation's *special issue on the first anniversary of the September 11, 2001, attacks.*

All history, the saying goes, is contemporary history. People instinctively turn to the past to help understand the present. Events draw our attention to previously neglected historical subjects. The second wave of feminism gave birth to a flourishing subfield of women's history. The Reagan revolution spawned a cottage industry in the history of US conservatism.

Many years will pass before we can fully assess how our thinking about history has changed as a result of September 11. While historians ponder this question, conservative ideologues have produced a spate of polemical statements on how we should teach American history in light of recent events. In a speech less than a month after the tragedy, Lynne Cheney insisted that calls for more intensive study of the rest of the world amounted to blaming America's "failure to understand Islam" for the attack.

A letter distributed by the American Council of Trustees and Alumni, which she once chaired, chastised professors who fail to teach the "truth" that civilization itself "is best exemplified in the West and indeed in America."

In *What's So Great About America*, Dinesh D'Souza contends that freedom and religious toleration are uniquely "Western" beliefs. The publisher's ad for the book identifies those who hold alternative views as "people who provide a rationale for terrorism." With funding from conservative foundations and powerful political connections, such commentators hope to reshape the teaching of American history.

Historians cannot predict the future, but the past they portray must be one from which the present can plausibly have grown. The self-absorbed, super-celebratory history now being promoted will not enable students to make sense of either their own society or our increasingly interconnected world.

Historians cannot choose the ways history becomes part of our own experience. September 11 has rudely placed certain issues at the forefront of our consciousness. Let me mention three and their implications for how we think about the American past: the upsurge of patriotism, significant infringements on civil liberties and a sudden awareness of considerable distrust abroad of American actions and motives.

The generation of historians that came of age during the Vietnam War witnessed firsthand how patriotic language and symbols, especially the American flag, can be invoked in the service of manifestly unjust causes. Partly as a result, they have tended to neglect the power of these symbols as genuine expressions of a sense of common national community. Patriotism, if studied at all, has been understood as an "invention," rather than a habit of the heart.

Historians have had greater success lately at dividing up the American past into discrete experiences delineated along lines of race, ethnicity, gender and class than at exploring the common threads of American nationality. But the immediate response to September 11 cut across these boundaries. No one knows if the renewed sense of common purpose and shared national identity that surfaced so vividly after September 11 will prove temporary. But they require historians to devote new attention to the roots of the symbols, values and experiences Americans share as well as those that divide them.

All patriotic upsurges run the risk of degenerating into a coercive drawing of boundaries between "loyal" Americans and those stigmatized as aliens and traitors. This magazine has chronicled the numerous and disturbing infringements on civil liberties that have followed September 11. Such legal protections as habeas corpus, trial by impartial jury, the right to legal representation and equality before the law regardless of race or national origin have been seriously curtailed.

Civil liberties have been severely abridged during previous moments of crisis, from the Alien and Sedition Acts of 1798 to Japanese-American internment in World War II. Historians generally view these past episodes as shameful anomalies. But we are now living through another such episode, and there is a remarkable absence of public outcry.

We need an American history that sees protections for civil liberties not as a timeless feature of our "civilization" but as a recent and fragile achievement resulting from many decades of historical struggle. We should take a new look at obscure Supreme Court cases—*Fong Yue Ting* (1893), the Insular Cases of the early twentieth century, *Korematsu* during World War II— in which the justices allowed the government virtual carte blanche in dealing with aliens and in suspending the rights of specific groups of citizens on grounds of military necessity. Dissenting in *Fong Yue Ting*, which authorized the deportation of Chinese immigrants without due process, Justice David Brewer observed that, like today, the power was directed against a people many Americans found "obnoxious." But, he warned, "who shall say it will not be exercised tomorrow against other classes and other people?"

September 11 will also undoubtedly lead historians to examine more closely the history of the country's relationship with the larger world. Public opinion polls revealed that few Americans have any knowledge of other peoples' grievances against the United States. A study of our history in its inter-national context might help to explain why there is widespread fear outside our borders that the "war on terror" is motivated in part by the desire to impose a Pax Americana in a grossly unequal world.

Back in the 1930s, historian Herbert Bolton warned that by treating the American past in isolation, historians were helping to raise up a "nation of chauvinists"—a danger worth remembering when considering the drumbeat of calls for a celebratory and insular history divorced from its global context. Of course, international paradigms can be every bit as obfuscating as histories that are purely national. We must be careful not to reproduce traditional American exceptionalism on a global scale.

September 11, for example, has inspired a spate of commentary influenced by Samuel Huntington's mid-1990s book *The Clash of Civilizations*. Huntington's paradigm reduces politics and culture to a single characteristic—race, religion or geography—that remains forever static, divorced from historical development or change through interaction with other societies. It makes it impossible to discuss divisions within these purported civilizations. The idea that the West is the sole home of reason, liberty and tolerance ignores how recently such values triumphed in the United States and also ignores the debates over creationism, abortion rights and other issues that suggest that commitment to them is hardly unanimous. The definition of "Western civilization" is highly selective—it includes the Enlightenment but not the Inquisition, liberalism but not the Holocaust, Charles Darwin but not the Salem witch trials.

Nor can September 11 be explained by reference to timeless characteristics or innate pathologies of "Islamic civilization." From the Ku Klux Klan during Reconstruction to Oklahoma City in our own time, our society has produced its own homegrown terrorists. Terrorism springs from specific historical causes, not the innate qualities of one or another civilization.

The study of history should transcend boundaries rather than reinforce or reproduce them. In the wake of September 11, it is all the more imperative that the history we teach be a candid appraisal of our society's strengths and weaknesses, not simply an exercise in self-celebration—a conversation with the entire world, not a complacent dialogue with ourselves. ❖

None Dare Call It Treason

JUNE 2, 2003

Few traditions are more American than freedom of speech and the right to dissent. But an equally powerful American tradition has been the effort by government and private "patriots" to suppress free expression in times of crisis. During the fighting in Iraq, former military leaders who criticized planning for the war were denounced for endangering troops in the field and warned to remain silent. A number of scholars, including myself, were branded "Traitor Professors" on a television talk show. If criticism of a war while it is in progress makes one a traitor, that category will have to include Abraham Lincoln, who denounced the Mexican War while serving in Congress in 1847; Mark Twain, who vehemently attacked government policy in the Spanish-American and Philippine wars at the turn of the last century; and Martin Luther King Jr., who eloquently called for an end to the war in Vietnam.

With the exception of World War II, every significant war in American history has inspired vigorous dissent. Many colonists remained loyal to Britain during the American Revolution.

Most New Englanders opposed the War of 1812. Numerous Americans considered the Mexican War an effort to extend the territory of slavery. Both North and South were internally divided during the Civil War. World War I and Vietnam produced massive antiwar movements. This is part of our democratic tradition.

Equally persistent, however, have been efforts to suppress wartime dissent. The Alien and Sedition Acts during the "quasiwar" with France in 1798 allowed the president to deport aliens and made it illegal to criticize the government. Both Union and Confederate governments suppressed opposition newspapers and jailed critics. World War I witnessed a massive repression of freedom of speech, with critics of the war, socialists and labor leaders jailed or deported, those suspected of disloyalty rounded up by private vigilantes and the speaking of German banned in some places. Universities, including my own, fired professors who opposed American involvement.

Self-proclaimed patriots not only seek to determine the boundaries of acceptable speech about the present but rewrite history to create a more politically useful past. During World War I, the Committee on Public Information, a government propaganda agency, published pamphlets demonstrating the "common principles" of Oliver Cromwell, Jean-Jacques Rousseau and Thomas Jefferson in order to create a historical lineage for the Anglo-French-American military alliance. Today, statements about history that in normal times would seem uncontroversial have been labeled treasonous. Daniel Pipes said in his syndicated newspaper column that I "hate America" because I noted that Japan invoked the idea of pre-emptive war to justify its attack on

Pearl Harbor (a point also made by that well-known anti-American, Arthur Schlesinger Jr.). My comment to a reporter that the United States has frequently embarked on military ventures without being attacked, as in Haiti, the Dominican Republic and Vietnam, prompted accusations of treason in the media.

In the aftermath of the Civil War, a far greater crisis than the war on Iraq, the Supreme Court in the *Milligan* case invalidated the use of military tribunals to try civilians. The court proclaimed that the Constitution is not suspended in wartime: "It is a law for rulers and people, equally in war and in peace." Alas, we have not always lived up to this ideal. The history of civil liberties in the United States is not a straight-line trajectory toward ever-greater freedom. It is a complex story in which victories can prove temporary and regression can follow progress.

Our civil liberties are neither self-enforcing nor self-correcting. Historians today view past suppressions of free speech as shameful episodes. But we are now living through another moment when many commentators, both in and out of government, seem to view freedom of expression as at best an inconvenience and at worst unpatriotic. The incessant attacks on dissenters as traitors are intended to create an atmosphere of shock and awe within the United States, so that those tempted to speak their mind become too intimidated to do so.

George W. Bush has claimed that America's enemies wish to destroy our freedoms. If we surrender freedom of speech in the hope that this will bring swifter victory on current and future battlefields, who then will have won the war? ❖

Lincoln's Antiwar Record

An old marketing adage states that no product exists whose sales cannot be improved by associating it with Abraham Lincoln. The same seems to be true in politics. As Congress debated resolutions condemning the escalation of the Iraq War, the remaining supporters of George W. Bush's Iraq policy invoked Lincoln to tar the war's opponents with the brush of treason. But this reflects a complete misunderstanding of Lincoln's record.

The latest example of the misuse of Lincoln came in a February 13 article in the *Washington Times* by conservative writer Frank Gaffney. Gaffney quoted Lincoln as declaring that wartime congressmen who "damage morale and undermine the military" should be "exiled or hanged." Glenn Greenwald, on *Salon*, quickly pointed out that the "quote," which has circulated for the past few years in conservative circles, is a fabrication. (Conservative use of invented Lincoln statements is nothing new—Ronald Reagan used a series of them in a speech to the 1992 Republican National Convention. But today, when Lincoln's entire works are online and easily searchable, there is no possible excuse for invoking fraudulent quotations.)

Greenwald did not point out that Lincoln's record as a member of Congress during the Mexican War utterly refutes the conservative effort to appropriate his legacy. Lincoln was elected to the House of Representatives in 1846, shortly after President James Polk invaded Mexico when that country refused his demand to sell California to the United States. Polk falsely claimed that he was responding to a Mexican invasion.

Shortly before Lincoln's term in Congress began, he attended a speech in Lexington, Kentucky, by his political idol Senator Henry Clay. "This is no war of defense," Clay declared in a blistering attack on Polk, "but one of unnecessary and offensive aggression." A month later, Lincoln introduced a set of resolutions challenging Polk's contention that Mexico had shed American blood on American soil and voted for a statement, approved by the House, that declared the war "unnecessarily and unconstitutionally begun by the President."

Clay and Lincoln objected as strenuously as any member of Congress today to a war launched by a president on fabricated grounds. When Lincoln's law partner, William Herndon, defended the president's right to invade another country if he considered it threatening, Lincoln sent a devastating reply. Herndon, he claimed, would allow a president "to make war at pleasure. Study to see if you can fix *any limit* to his power in this respect. … If, to-day, he should choose to say he thinks it necessary to invade Canada, to prevent the British from invading us, how could you stop him?"

The Constitution, he went on, gave the "war-making power" to Congress precisely to prevent presidents from starting wars while "pretending ... that the good of the people was the object."

Like Bush, Lincoln spoke of the United States as a beacon of liberty, an example to the world of the virtues of democracy. But he rejected the idea of American aggression in the name of freedom. He included in an 1859 speech a biting satire of "Young America," a group of writers and politicians who glorified territorial aggrandizement. Young America, he remarked, "owns a large part of the world, by right of possessing it; and all the rest by right of *wanting* it, and *intending* to have it. ... He is a great friend of humanity; and his desire for land is not selfish, but merely an impulse to extend the area of freedom. He is very anxious to fight for the liberation of enslaved nations and colonies, provided, always, they *have* land." Substitute "oil" for "land" and the statement seems eerily relevant in the early twenty-first century.

Conservatives should think twice before invoking Lincoln's words, real or invented, in the cause of the Iraq War and before equating condemnations of Bush's policies and usurpations with treason. ❖

Our Lincoln

JANUARY 26, 2009

Abraham Lincoln has always provided a lens through which Americans examine themselves. He has been described as a consummate moralist and a shrewd political operator, a lifelong foe of slavery and an inveterate racist. Politicians from conservatives to communists, civil rights activists to segregationists, have claimed him as their own. With the approach of the bicentennial of his birth, the past few years have seen an outpouring of books on Lincoln of every size, shape and description. His psychology, marriage, law career, political practices, racial attitudes and every one of his major speeches have been subjected to minute examination.

Lincoln is important to us not because of his melancholia or how he chose his cabinet but because of his role in the vast human drama of emancipation and what his life tells us about slavery's enduring legacy. *The Nation*, founded by veterans of the struggle for abolition three months after Lincoln's death, dedicated itself to completing the unfinished task of making the former slaves equal citizens. It soon abandoned this goal, but in the twentieth century again took up the banner of racial justice. Who is *our* Lincoln?

In the wake of the 2008 election and an inaugural address with "a new birth of freedom," a phrase borrowed from the Gettysburg Address, as its theme, the Lincoln we should remember is the politician whose greatness lay in his capacity for growth. Much of that growth stemmed from his complex relationship with the radicals of his day, black and white abolitionists who fought against overwhelming odds to bring the moral issue of slavery to the forefront of national life.

Until well into the Civil War, Lincoln was not an advocate of immediate abolition. But he was well aware of the abolitionists' significance in creating public sentiment hostile to slavery. Every schoolboy, Lincoln noted in 1858, recognized the names of William Wilberforce and Granville Sharpe, leaders of the earlier struggle to outlaw the Atlantic slave trade, "but who can now name a single man who labored to retard it?" On issue after issue—abolition in the nation's capital, wartime emancipation, enlisting black soldiers, amending the Constitution to abolish slavery, allowing some blacks to vote—Lincoln came to occupy positions the abolitionists had first staked out. The destruction of slavery during the war offers an example, as relevant today as in Lincoln's time, of how the combination of an engaged social movement and an enlightened leader can produce progressive social change.

* * *

Unlike the abolitionists, most of whom sought to influence the political system from outside, for nearly his entire adult life

Lincoln was a politician. He first ran for the Illinois legislature at 23. Although he spoke occasionally about slavery during his early career, Lincoln did not elaborate his views until the 1850s, when he emerged as a major spokesman for the newly created Republican Party, committed to halting slavery's westward expansion. Like Barack Obama, Lincoln came to national prominence through oratory, not a record of significant accomplishment in office. In speeches of eloquence and power, Lincoln condemned slavery as a violation of the founding principles of the United States as enunciated in the Declaration of Independence—the affirmation of human equality and of the natural right to life, liberty and the pursuit of happiness.

"I have always hated slavery," Lincoln once declared, "I think as much as any abolitionist." He spoke of slavery as a "monstrous injustice," a cancer that threatened the lifeblood of the American nation. But he did not share the abolitionist conviction that the moral issue of slavery overrode all others. William Lloyd Garrison burned a copy of the Constitution because of its clauses protecting slavery. But Lincoln, as he explained in a letter to his Kentucky friend Joshua Speed, was willing to "crucify [his] feelings" out of "loyalty to the Constitution and the Union."

Like many of his contemporaries, Lincoln believed the United States embodied the principles of democracy and self-government and should help to spread them throughout the world. This, of course, was the theme of the Gettysburg Address. He was not, to be sure, a believer in Manifest Destiny—the idea that Americans had a God-given right to acquire new territory in the name of liberty, regardless of the desires of the territory's actual inhabitants. Lincoln saw American democracy as an example to the rest of the world, not something to be imposed by unilateral force. Slavery interfered with the fulfillment of this historic mission: It "deprives our republican example of its just influence in the world—enables the enemies of free institutions, with plausibility, to taunt us as hypocrites—causes the real friends of freedom to doubt our sincerity." Yet, for the United States to serve as a beacon of democracy, the nation's unity must be maintained, even if this meant compromising with slavery.

Another key difference between Lincoln and abolitionists lay in their views regarding race. Abolitionists insisted that once freed, slaves should be recognized as equal members of the Republic. They viewed the struggles against slavery and racism as intimately connected. Lincoln saw them as distinct. Unlike his Democratic opponents in the North and pro-slavery advocates in the South, Lincoln claimed for blacks the natural rights enumerated in the Declaration of Independence. But, he insisted, these did not necessarily carry with them civil, political or social equality. Persistently charged with belief in "Negro equality" during his campaign for the Senate against Stephen Douglas in 1858, Lincoln responded that he was not, "nor ever have been, in favor of making voters or jurors of Negroes, nor of qualifying them to hold office, nor to intermarry with white people." Abolitionists worked tirelessly to repeal Northern laws that relegated blacks to second-class citizenship. Lincoln refused to condemn the notorious Black Laws of Illinois, which made it a crime for black people to enter the state.

Throughout the 1850s and for the first half of the Civil War, Lincoln believed that "colonization"—that is, encouraging black people to emigrate to a new homeland in Africa, the Caribbean or Central America—ought to accompany the end of slavery. We sometimes forget how widespread the belief in colonization was in the pre–Civil War era. Henry Clay and Thomas Jefferson, the statesmen most revered by Lincoln, outlined plans to accomplish it. Colonization allowed its proponents to think about the end of slavery without confronting the question of the place of blacks in a post-emancipation society. Some colonizationists spoke of the "degradation" of free blacks and insisted that multiplying their numbers would pose a danger to American society. Others, like Lincoln, emphasized the strength of white racism. Because of it, he said several times, blacks could never achieve equality in the United States. They should remove themselves to a homeland where they could fully enjoy freedom and self-government.

Colonization was bitterly opposed by most blacks in the North, and, after 1830, by most white abolitionists. They offered an alternative vision of America as a biracial society of equals. Through the attack on colonization, the modern idea of equality as something that knows no racial boundaries was born. At the time of his election as president, however, Lincoln was typical of the majority of Northerners, who were willing to go to war over slavery's expansion yet thought of America as essentially a country for white people.

Lincoln shared many of the prevailing prejudices of his era. But, he insisted, there was a bedrock principle of equality that transcended race—the equal right to the fruits of one's labor. There are many grounds for condemning the institution of slavery: moral, religious, political, economic. Lincoln referred to all of them at one time or another. But ultimately he saw slavery as a form of theft, of one person appropriating the labor of another. Using a black woman as an illustration, he explained the kind of equality in which he believed: "In some respects she certainly is not my equal; but in her natural right to eat the bread she earns with her own hands without asking leave of any one else, she is my equal, and the equal of all others."

Shortly before the 1860 election, Frederick Douglass offered a succinct summary of the dilemma confronting opponents of slavery like Lincoln, who worked within the political system rather than outside it. Abstractly, Douglass wrote, most Northerners would agree that slavery was wrong. The challenge was to find a way of "translating antislavery sentiment into antislavery action." The Constitution barred interference with slavery in the states where it already existed. For Lincoln, as for most Republicans, antislavery action meant not attacking slavery where it was but working to prevent slavery's westward expansion.

Lincoln, however, did talk about a future without slavery. The aim of the Republican Party, he insisted, was to put the institution on the road to "ultimate extinction," a phrase he borrowed from Henry Clay. Ultimate extinction could take a long time: Lincoln once said that slavery might survive for another hundred years. But to the South, Lincoln seemed as dangerous as an abolitionist, because he was committed to the eventual end of slavery. This was why his election in 1860 led inexorably to secession and civil war.

* * *

The war did not begin as a crusade to abolish slavery. Almost from the start, however, abolitionists and Radical Republicans pressed for action against the institution as a war measure. And very quickly, slavery began to disintegrate. Hundreds, then thousands, of blacks ran away to Union lines. Far from the battlefields, reports multiplied of insubordinate behavior. The actions of slaves forced the administration to begin to devise policies with regard to slavery.

Faced with this pressure, Lincoln put forward his own ideas. He first proposed gradual, voluntary emancipation coupled with monetary compensation for slaveholders and colonization of freed blacks—the traditional approach of politicians critical of slavery but unwilling to challenge the property right of slaveholders. Lincoln's plan would make slaveowners partners in abolition. He suggested it to the four slave states that remained in the Union—Delaware, Maryland, Kentucky and Missouri—but found no takers. In mid-1862 Congress moved ahead of Lincoln on emancipation, although he signed all its measures: abolition in the territories; abolition in the District of Columbia (with around $300 compensation for each owner); the Second Confiscation Act of July 1862, which freed all slaves of pro-Confederate owners in areas henceforth occupied by the Union Army and slaves of such owners who escaped to Union lines.

Meanwhile, Lincoln was moving toward a new approach to slavery. A powerful combination of events propelled him: the failure of efforts to fight the Civil War without targeting the economic foundation of Southern society; the need to forestall threatened British recognition of the Confederacy; mounting demands in the North for abolition; and the waning of enthusiasm for military enlistment, which sparked a desire to tap the reservoir of black manpower for the military. In September 1862 Lincoln warned the South to lay down its arms or face a presidential decree abolishing slavery. On January 1, 1863, he signed the Emancipation Proclamation.

Contrary to legend, Lincoln did not free 4 million slaves with a stroke of his pen. A measure whose constitutional legitimacy rested on the "war power" of the president, the proclamation had no bearing on slaves in the four border states that remained in the Union. It also exempted certain areas of the Confederacy under Union military control. All told, the Emancipation Proclamation did not apply to perhaps 750,000 of the 4 million slaves.

Unlike the Declaration of Independence, the proclamation contains no soaring language, no immortal preamble enunciating the rights of man. Nonetheless, it marked the turning point of the Civil War and of Lincoln's understanding of his role in history. The proclamation sounded the death knell of slavery in the United States. Everybody recognized that if slavery perished in South Carolina, Alabama and Mississippi, it could hardly survive in Kentucky, Missouri and a few parishes of Louisiana.

In his annual message to Congress of December 1862, Lincoln pointed out that crises require Americans to rethink their previous assumptions: "As our case is new, so we must think anew, and act anew. We must disenthrall ourselves, and then we shall save our country." Lincoln included himself in that "we." The Emancipation Proclamation was markedly different from his previous statements and policies regarding slavery. It was immediate, not gradual, contained no mention of monetary compensation for slaveowners and made no reference to colonization. Instead, it enjoined emancipated slaves to "labor faithfully for reasonable wages" in the United States. For the first time, it authorized the enrollment of black soldiers into the Union Army. The proclamation set in motion the process by which 200,000 black men in the last two years of the war fought for the Union. Putting black men into the military implied a very different vision of their future place in American society than earlier plans for settling freed slaves overseas.

Lincoln came to emancipation more slowly than the abolitionists and their Radical Republican allies desired. But having made the decision, he did not look back. In 1864, with casualties mounting, some urged him to rescind the proclamation, in which case, they believed, the South could be persuaded to return to the Union. Lincoln would not consider this. Were he to do so, he told one visitor, "I should be damned in time and eternity." Indeed, in the last two years of the war, he pressed the border states to take action against slavery on their own, and made support of emancipation a requirement for Southerners who renounced the Confederacy and wished to have their property other than slaves restored. He worked to secure Congressional passage of the Thirteenth Amendment. This was another measure originally proposed by the abolitionists that Lincoln came to support. When ratified in 1865, it marked the irrevocable destruction of slavery throughout the United States.

Moreover, by decoupling emancipation from colonization, Lincoln in effect launched the process known as Reconstruction— the remaking of Southern society, politics and race relations. Lincoln did not live to see it implemented and eventually abandoned. But in the last two years of the war he came to recognize that if emancipation settled one question, the fate of slavery, it opened another: What was to be the role of emancipated slaves in postwar American life? The "new birth of freedom" ushered in by the war was one in which blacks for the first time would share. During Reconstruction this would entail a redefinition of American nationality—the rewriting of the laws and Constitution to embrace the abolitionist vision of a society that had advanced beyond the tyranny of race.

In 1863 and 1864, Lincoln for the first time began to think seriously of the role blacks would play in a postslavery America. In his "last speech," delivered at the White House in April 1865 a few days before his assassination, Lincoln announced his support for limited black suffrage in the reconstructed South. He singled out as most worthy the "very intelligent"—educated blacks who had been free before the war—and "those who serve our cause as soldiers." Hardly an unambiguous embrace of equality, this was the first time an American president had publicly endorsed any kind of political rights for blacks (this at a time when only six Northern states allowed blacks to vote). Lincoln was telling the country that the service of black soldiers entitled them to a voice in the reunited nation.

A month earlier, Lincoln had looked to the future in perhaps his greatest speech of all, the Second Inaugural Address. Today we tend to remember it for its closing words: "with malice toward none, with charity for all … let us strive to bind up the nation's wounds." But before that noble ending, Lincoln tried to instruct his fellow countrymen on the historical significance of the war and the unfinished task that lay ahead.

It must have been very tempting, with Union victory imminent, for Lincoln to blame the sins of the Confederacy for the war and claim the outcome as the will of God. Everybody knew, he noted, that slavery was "somehow" the cause of the war. Yet Lincoln called it "American slavery," not Southern slavery, underscoring the entire nation's complicity. No man, he continued, knows God's will. God might wish the war to continue as a punishment for the sin of slavery, "until all the wealth piled by the bondman's two hundred and fifty years of unrequited toil shall be sunk, and until every drop of blood drawn with the lash, shall be paid by another drawn by the sword." For one last time, he reiterated his definition of slavery as the theft of labor, now coupled with one of his very few public invocations of the physical brutality inherent in the institution (he generally preferred to appeal to the reason of his listeners rather than their emotions).

In essence, Lincoln was asking Americans to confront unblinkingly the legacy of bondage and to think about the requirements of justice. What is the nation's obligation for those 250 years of unpaid labor? What is necessary to enable the former slaves, their children and their descendants to enjoy the "pursuit of happiness" he had always insisted was their natural right but that had so long been denied them? Lincoln did not live to provide an answer.

Today we inhabit an entirely different world from Lincoln's. But the questions raised by emancipation continue to bedevil American society. The challenge confronting President Obama is to move beyond the powerful symbolism of his election as the first African-American president toward substantive actions that address the still unfinished struggle for equality. ❖

The Professional

The first year may not be the best way to judge a president. After one year in office, Abraham Lincoln still insisted that slavery would not become a target of the Union war effort, Franklin D. Roosevelt had yet to address the need for social insurance in the wake of the Great Depression and John F. Kennedy viewed the civil rights movement as an annoying distraction. If we admire them today, it is mostly for what happened during the rest of their presidencies.

Nonetheless, it is difficult to view Obama's initial year without a feeling of deep disappointment. This arises from more than unrealistic expectations, although his candidacy certainly aroused a great deal of wishful thinking among those yearning for a change after nearly thirty years of Reaganism. Nor does disappointment result from too exacting a standard of judgment. In fact, the bar has arguably been set too low. Too many of us have been willing to fall back on a comparison between Obama and his predecessor, arguably the worst president in American history, and leave it at that.

Not surprisingly, given the global economic crisis, numerous observers greeted Obama's election by comparing him to FDR. This was a serious error. Obama is not a New Deal liberal. Rather, his outlook reflects how the preoccupations of liberalism have changed under the impact of the social and political transformations since the 1930s.

Obama came of age politically at a time when the decline of the labor movement had eroded one social base of liberalism while new ones were emerging from the upheavals of the 1960s and the changing racial and ethnic composition of the American population. Personally, he embodies the rise to prominence in the Democratic Party of highly educated professionals, including a new black upper middle class that emerged from the struggles of the '60s and subsequent affirmative action programs. He is also closely identified with what might be called the more forward-looking wing of Wall Street, which contributed heavily to his campaign and to which he has entrusted his economic policy.

Obama has no evident desire to address the questions that defined New Deal liberalism and remain all too relevant today— economic inequality; mass unemployment; unrestrained corporate power; and the struggle of workers, through unions, to enjoy "industrial democracy." Where Obama has been good is on issues that were subordinate themes during the 1930s but have become central to post–World War II liberalism—women's reproductive rights, respect for civil liberties and the rule of law, environmentalism and racial and ethnic diversity, especially in government employment.

Obama also embodies a strain of thought alien to the New Deal but associated with the Progressivism of the early twentieth century, the desire to take politics out of the hands of politicians. Like the old Progressives, he seems to believe that the government can move beyond partisan politics to operate in a businesslike manner to promote the public good (despite clear evidence that the other side is not cooperating). As in the Progressive Era, this outlook goes hand in hand with a strong respect for scientific expertise (quite different from George W. Bush's approach).

Listing these characteristics of Obama's thinking makes it clear that the president he most resembles is not FDR or Abraham Lincoln, as was frequently suggested before his inauguration, but Jimmy Carter. Like Carter, Obama seems to view economic globalization and American deindustrialization as an inevitable process and to see the role of government as seeking to mitigate their destructive impact. Like Carter, he has gone out of his way to appoint a racially diverse administration. Like Carter, he does not have an industrial policy or a robust jobs-creation program and seems uninterested in addressing the hardships and structural imbalances caused by the decline of manufacturing.

* * *

Obama's economic program reflects and, indeed, reinforces the long-term shift from manufacturing to finance in the American economy. And his bailout of the banks and insurance megacompany AIG with no strings attached has aroused resentments that should not be ignored, even if they are often couched in extreme and racist language. There is a widespread sense that the rules of the game have been fixed to the advantage of the wealthy and that the government is indifferent to the plight of ordinary Americans. Ironically, for all the blacks appointed to highly visible positions in Washington, the condition of most African-Americans has worsened during Obama's first year. Blacks have suffered disproportionately from the decline of manufacturing employment and mortgage foreclosures. It is unlikely that an avowedly post-racial president will directly address their plight.

On foreign policy, the parallels with Carter are even closer, down to a joint preoccupation with Afghanistan. Both Carter and Obama reoriented the rhetoric of American foreign policy toward international cooperation, yet found it difficult to translate this ideal into practice. Carter continued to support tyrants like the Shah of Iran, launched a military buildup that paved the way for Reagan's and reinvigorated the Cold War after the Soviet occupation of Afghanistan. As for Obama, his recent address on Afghanistan and his surprisingly bellicose speech accepting the Nobel Peace Prize reveal that he has comfortably embraced the role of wartime president, even adopting Bush-like language about a titanic global confrontation between the forces of evil and those of freedom. This has reignited the martial spirit of the liberal interventionists, who applauded the invasion of Iraq, later apologized (more or less) and now praise Obama's supposed "realism" in recognizing that wars are sometimes necessary. Only "just wars," of course. But was there ever a war its combatants did not consider just?

* * *

One lesson we should learn from Obama's first year is the difficulty of effecting change, even in times of crisis. Fearful of popular democracy, the men who wrote the Constitution created a government system designed to make it far easier to prevent change than to implement it. Today this structural inertia is compounded by the power of money in politics and by an entrenched military establishment. Obama has failed to heed the lesson Kennedy learned from the Bay of Pigs debacle at the outset of his presidency—not to accept at face value the advice of his generals (a realization that served Kennedy and the world well during the Cuban missile confrontation of 1962).

* * *

A crisis, however, also creates an opportunity. To seize it, the first prerequisite is to "disenthrall ourselves" from accepted maxims, as Lincoln urged Americans to do in 1862. "As our case is new," he said, "so we must think anew and act anew." Obama still has plenty of time to do this. It was only after their first year that Lincoln became the Great Emancipator, FDR the architect of the Second New Deal and Kennedy a champion of civil rights. Not one of these presidents acted simply on his own volition. All three were pressured to change by engaged social movements—abolitionists, the labor movement, the struggle for racial justice.

Given this country's tortured racial history, Obama's election will always represent a symbolic watershed. To make sure that it amounts to more than this, progressives must stop making excuses or falling back on extenuating circumstances in assessing Obama. Without forgetting the differences between Obama and his increasingly retrograde Republican opposition, we must reject the outdated assumptions to which Obama clings on economic and foreign policy and forthrightly press for genuine change, speaking truth to power even when that power is held by men and women we helped put into office. ❖

Zinn's Critical History

Friedrich Nietzsche once identified three approaches to the writing of history: the monumental, the antiquarian and the critical, the last being history "that judges and condemns." Howard Zinn, who died on January 27 at 87, wrote the third kind. Unlike many historians, he was not afraid to speak out about the difference between right and wrong.

Zinn was best known, of course, as the author of *A People's History of the United States*, which since its publication in 1980 has introduced millions of readers to his vision of the American past. Few historians manage to reach a broad nonacademic audience. Those who do generally write Nietzsche's monumental history, works that celebrate great men (the founding fathers, Abraham Lincoln) or heroic events (the building of the Transcontinental Railroad, World War II). Zinn's history was different. Through *A People's History* and various spinoffs (including a recent dramatization by prominent actors of a collection of documents on the History Channel), Zinn's public learned about ordinary Americans' struggles for justice, equality and power.

I have long been struck by how many excellent students of history first had their passion for the past sparked by reading Howard Zinn. Sometimes, to be sure, his account tended toward the Manichaean, an oversimplified narrative of the battle between the forces of light and darkness. But *A People's History* taught an inspiring and salutary lesson—that despite all too frequent repression, if America has a history to celebrate it lies in the social movements that have made this a better country. As for past heroes, Zinn insisted, one should look not to presidents or captains of industry but to radicals such as Frederick Douglass, Susan B. Anthony and Eugene V. Debs.

Before writing *A People's History*, Zinn published *SNCC: The New Abolitionists* (1964). This book grew out of his experience teaching at Spelman College, an institution for young black women in Atlanta, and his participation in the civil rights movement. It remains essential reading for anyone seeking to understand the upheavals of the '60s. Its subtitle is worth noting. At a time when most historians still depicted nineteenth-century abolitionists as neurotic misfits whose agitation brought on an unnecessary war, Zinn identified their campaign against slavery as the beginning of a long, unfinished struggle for racial justice.

A veteran of World War II, Zinn spoke frequently about the horrors of war, lending his voice to those opposed to American involvement in Vietnam and, more recently, Iraq and Afghanistan. He was a passionate critic of the national security system and the militarization of American life.

A few years ago, I lectured at St. Olaf College in Northfield, Minnesota (the hometown of the late, lamented Senator Paul Wellstone). Zinn had been there a few days before, and across the top of the student newspaper was emblazoned the headline Zinn Attacks State. I sent Howard a copy. We laughingly agreed that he could not have a more appropriate epitaph. ✤

Twisting History in Texas

APRIL 5, 2010

The changes to the social studies curriculum recently approved by the conservative-dominated Texas Board of Education have attracted attention mainly because of how they may affect textbooks used in other states. Since Texas certifies texts centrally rather than by individual school districts, publishers have a strong incentive to alter their books to conform to its standards so as to reach the huge Texas market. Where was Lee Harvey Oswald, after all, when he shot John F. Kennedy? In the Texas School Book Depository—a tall Dallas building filled with textbooks.

Most comment on the content of the new standards has focused on the mandate that high school students learn about leading conservative figures and institutions of the 1980s and '90s, specifically Phyllis Schlafly, the Moral Majority, the Heritage Foundation, the Contract With America and the NRA. In fact, there is nothing wrong with teaching about modern conservatism, a key force in recent American history. My own textbook has a chapter called "The Triumph of Conservatism" and discusses most of the individuals and groups mentioned above.

More interesting is what the new standards tell us about conservatives' overall vision of American history and society and how they hope to instill that vision in the young. The standards run from kindergarten through high school, and certain themes obsessively recur. Judging from the updated social studies curriculum, conservatives want students to come away from a Texas education with a favorable impression of: women who adhere to traditional gender roles, the Confederacy, some parts of the Constitution, capitalism, the military and religion. They do not think students should learn about women who demanded greater equality; other parts of the Constitution; slavery, Reconstruction and the unequal treatment of nonwhites generally; environmentalists; labor unions; federal economic regulation; or foreigners.

Here are a few examples. The board has removed mention of the Declaration of the Seneca Falls Convention, the letters of John and Abigail Adams and suffrage advocate Carrie Chapman Catt. As examples of "good citizenship" for third graders, it deleted Harriet Tubman and included Clara Barton, founder of the Red Cross, and Helen Keller (the board seems to have slipped up here—Keller was a committed socialist). The role of religion—but not the separation of church and state—receives emphasis throughout. For example, religious revivals are now listed as one of the twelve major "events and eras" from colonial days to 1877.

The changes seek to reduce or elide discussion of slavery, mentioned mainly for its "impact" on different regions and the coming of the Civil War. A reference to the Atlantic slave trade is dropped in favor of "Triangular trade." Jefferson Davis's inaugural address as president of the Confederacy will now be studied alongside Abraham Lincoln's speeches.

In grade one, Veterans Day replaces Martin Luther King Jr. Day in the list of holidays students should be familiar with. (Later, "building a military" has been added as one of two results of the Revolution—the other being the creation of the United States—an odd inclusion, given the founders' fear of a standing army.) The Double-V Campaign during World War II (blacks' demand that victory over the Axis powers be accompanied by victory over segregation at home) has been omitted from the high school curriculum. Japanese-American internment is now juxtaposed with "the regulation of some foreign nationals," ignoring the fact that while a few Germans and Italians were imprisoned as enemy aliens, the vast majority of people of Japanese ancestry who were interned were US citizens.

Students in several grades will be required to understand the "benefits" (but none of the drawbacks) of capitalism. The economic system, however, dares not speak its name—it is referred to throughout as "free enterprise." Labor unions are conspicuous by their absence. Mankind's impact on the environment is apparently entirely benign—the curriculum mentions dams for flood control and the benefits of transportation infrastructure but none of the problems arising from the exploitation of nature. Lest anyone think that Americans should not fall below a rudimentary standard of living, the kindergarten curriculum deletes food, shelter and clothing from its list of "basic human needs."

Americans, the board seems to suggest, do not need to take much notice of the rest of the world, or of noncitizens in this country. Kindergartners no longer have to learn about "people" who have contributed to American life, only about "patriots and good citizens." High school students must evaluate the pros and cons of US participation in "international organizations and treaties." In an original twist, third grade geography students no longer have to be able to identify on a map the Amazon, the Himalayas or (as if it were in another country) Washington, DC.

Clearly, the Texas Board of Education seeks to inculcate children with a history that celebrates the achievements of our past while ignoring its shortcomings, and that largely ignores those who have struggled to make this a fairer, more equal society. I have lectured on a number of occasions to Texas precollege teachers and have found them as competent, dedicated and open-minded as the best teachers anywhere. But if they are required to adhere to the revised curriculum, the students of our second most populous state will emerge ill prepared for life in Texas, America and the world in the twenty-first century. ❖

Remembering Eric Hobsbawm

Eric Hobsbawm, who died on October 1 at the age of ninety-five, was perhaps the twentieth century's pre-eminent historian and a life-long advocate of social justice. Born in Alexandria, Egypt, in 1917 to a British father and Austrian mother, he was educated in Vienna and Berlin. His family sent him to London in 1933 when Hitler came to power and he lived for the rest of his life in England, where he taught for many years at London's Birkbeck College.

As a teenager, Hobsbawm not only witnessed the rise of Nazism but was present in 1936 at the massive popular demonstration in Paris that celebrated the electoral victory of the Popular Front. The events of that turbulent time led him to join the Communist Party and he remained a member until its disappearance in the 1990s, mostly, he wrote, out of respect for the memory of comrades who had suffered persecution or death for their political beliefs.

Hobsbawm's historical writings brought to bear a sophisticated Marxist analysis that saw class conflict as a driving force of historical change but rejected narrow economic determinism and teleological frameworks. Like Marx himself, Hobsbawm saw capitalism as a total social system, which had to be analyzed in its entirety, and rejected notions of historical inevitability. He insisted that people must strive to envision a more humane social order, but that history had no predetermined trajectory. His 1978 essay "The Forward March of Labour Halted?" offered a prescient and disturbing warning that the postwar expansion of social democracy and the power of organized labor, considered irreversible by many leftists, had reached a crisis point. His writings on the history of British labor helped to launch the "new social history" that dominated historical scholarship in Britain and the United States in the 1970s and 1980s. Yet in an influential 1971 essay, "From Social History to the History of Society," he warned that studies of the agency of ordinary people, so important in expanding the cast of historical characters, must be placed in the broader context of how social and political power is exercised.

Hobsbawm's books cover an amazing range of subjects. He first came to prominence in the 1950s with his contribution to what was then a lively debate over the "general crisis" of seventeenth-century England. Along with E. P. Thompson's *The Making of the English Working Class*, Hobsbawm's writings such as *Labouring Men* (1964) and *Primitive Rebels* (1959) helped to inspire the expansion of labor history from studies of trade unions to the examination of workers' lives, and sparked an interest in banditry, rural anarchism and other forms of what he called "prepolitical" protest. His economic history of modern Britain,

Industry and Empire (1968), remains a brilliant account of an epic economic transformation. He also wrote a wide-ranging study of nationalism in the modern world, *Nations and Nationalism Since 1780* (1990).

But Hobsbawm is best known for his magisterial four-volume series *The Age of Revolution* (1962), *The Age of Capital* (1975), *The Age of Empire* (1987) and *The Age of Extremes* (1994), which together chronicles world history from the beginning of the French Revolution to the end of the Soviet Union. Long before the current vogue for "internationalizing" the study of history, Hobsbawm insisted that capitalism is a global system, which must be studied in a global context. The books drew on events in every region of the world, and on sources and scholarship in multiple languages. Hobsbawm was comfortable discussing subjects as far afield from Great Britain as the Latin American wars of independence, the Meiji Restoration in Japan and the rise to global power of the United States, yet he was able to merge local details into a coherent account of global political, economic and social change. The account also delves into art, culture, science, technology and other realms of human creativity and experience. These books remain the starting point for anyone who seeks a comprehensive history of the modern world.

In 1952, Hobsbawm helped to found *Past and Present*, which became the world's most influential English-language historical journal. Its board included many Marxist scholars—Christopher Hill, E. P. Thompson and others—who left the Communist Party in the wake of 1956. Hobsbawm, as noted above, did not follow them out of the party, but he made his intellectual home with them. He remained on the editorial board until his death.

A polymath, Hobsbawm was also a noted jazz critic, for many years writing music reviews under the name Francis Newton. He was an accomplished essayist on current affairs, whose writings had a wide readership among those interested in British politics. In whatever genre, his works were lucid and powerful, and always carried a moral inflection.

Personally, Hobsbawm was a gregarious, open-minded and generous person, whose large circle of friends ranged across the political and social spectrum. I first met him in 1973 when, soon after receiving my doctorate, I spent a year conducting research in England. Hobsbawm invited me to attend the seminar on social history he directed at the Institute of Historical Research in London; in those meetings his sparkling intellect was on full display. Last summer, I attended his ninety-fifth-birthday party in London. This unforgettable occasion brought together family members, historians, political commentators, musicians and others. Confined to a wheelchair because of a fall, Hobsbawm's mind was as alert as ever. He delivered moving reminiscences about his life, dwelling especially on his long marriage to his wife, Marlene.

Hobsbawm's final book, *How to Change the World*, was published last year. His life and writings will long serve as an inspiration to those who believe that a knowledge of history is essential to understanding the current world, and to the struggle to create a better one. ❖

The Civil War in "Postracial" America

I n 1877, soon after retiring as president, Ulysses S. Grant embarked on a two-year tour of the world. At almost every location he was greeted with adulation. In London, the Duke of Wellington, whose father had vanquished Napoleon, praised Grant as a military genius, the architect of victory in one of the greatest wars known to human history. In Newcastle, tens of thousands of parading English workers, arrayed with the banners of their various crafts, hailed him as the man who had saved the world's leading experiment in democratic self-government and as a Hero of Freedom for his role in the emancipation of America's slaves. In Berlin, Otto von Bismarck, the chancellor of Germany, welcomed Grant as a nation-builder who had accomplished something on the battlefield—national unity—that Bismarck was attempting to create for his own people. "You had to save the Union," Bismarck commented, "just as we had to save Germany."

Grant's contemporaries recognized the Civil War as an event of international significance. One hundred and fifty years after the conflict began, the meanings they ascribed to it offer a useful way of outlining why it was so pivotal in our own history. The Civil War changed the nature of warfare, gave rise to an empowered nation-state, vindicated the idea of free labor and destroyed the modern world's greatest slave society. Each of these outcomes laid the foundation for the country we live in today. But as with all great historical events, each outcome carried with it ambiguous, even contradictory, consequences.

Because of the war, the nation survived. Yet in its physical destruction and massive loss of life (620,000 Americans, the equivalent of 6 million in today's population) and encouragement of a patriotism that equated criticism of the government with treason, the Civil War can be seen as an ominous harbinger of twentieth-century total war, with its erasure of the distinction between civilian and military targets and serious infringements on civil liberties at home.

The nation-state created by the war, Abraham Lincoln insisted, embodied the principle of self-government. But it could also be used for undemocratic purposes. Shortly after the guns fell silent, Treasurer Francis Spinner (whose signature adorned every greenback issued by the federal government—the first national currency and itself a symbol of expanded national power) observed: "The thing to be feared now is that we will be running around the world with a chip on our shoulder. If we can avoid this, a glorious future is ours." Just as Spinner feared, the reunited nation soon embarked on a career of imperial expansion, beginning with the acquisition of Alaska two years after the war ended and culminating at the turn of the century in the conquest and annexation of Hawaii, the Philippines and Puerto Rico. Indeed, the abolition of slavery, an indisputably moral exercise of national power, gave new meaning to Jefferson's description of the United States as an "empire of liberty." No matter how violent or oppressive, American expansion now meant, by definition, the expansion of freedom—a rhetoric alive and well today.

The principle of free labor may have triumphed with the Union's victory, but the national banking system, high tariffs and other economic policies instituted by the Lincoln administration in an effort to mobilize the North's resources for war underpinned a long-lasting alliance between the Republican Party, the national state and an emerging class of industrial capitalists and financiers. Partly because of the war, Lincoln's America—the world of small shops and farms—gave way to an industrial leviathan. It was left to the Gilded Age labor movement to warn that a new industrial aristocracy had taken the place of the Slave Power as the enemy of ordinary working people.

Even abolition had mixed results. Long after the war ended, Lincoln and the emancipated slave would remain global symbols of universal liberty. But the new system of racial inequality that followed the overthrow of postwar Reconstruction seriously tarnished the idea that the Civil War had produced a new birth of freedom, as Lincoln claimed at Gettysburg.

What people choose to remember about the Civil War has always been tinged by politics. In his excellent book *Race and*

Reunion: The Civil War in American Memory, historian David Blight demonstrates that as soon as the war ended, debate over how to remember it began. Two understandings of the war, he argues, collided in late nineteenth-century America: an "emancipationist" vision that emphasized black freedom and equality as essential to the war's meaning, and a "reconciliationist" narrative that de-emphasized slavery and saw both sides as fighting for noble causes—the Union, on the part of the North; local rights and individual liberty, on the part of the South. By the turn of the century, as soldiers from North and South fought side by side in the Spanish-American War, the latter triumphed. The abandonment of the nation's commitment to equal rights for the former slaves was one basis on which former white antagonists could reunite. And the displacement of slavery from a central role in the war accorded with the new racial realities under Jim Crow.

Forgetting some aspects of the past is as much a part of historical understanding as remembering others. For decades it remained a cliché that the Confederacy lost the war on the battlefield but won the battle over historical memory. In the highly influential writings of Charles and Mary Beard early in the last century, the war was brought on by a conflict between industrial and agricultural elites, and slavery hardly deserved a footnote in the narrative. "Revisionist" historians of the 1920s, '30s and '40s, most of them Southern-born, insisted that slavery was a benign institution that would soon have died out peacefully. Thus, the Civil War was unnecessary—a "needless war" brought about by irresponsible fanatics (Northern abolitionists) who inflamed public passions and by a "blundering generation" of political leaders who failed to resolve eminently compromisable sectional differences. In black communities, the legacy of the 200,000 black men who fought in the Union army and navy remained alive. But the memory of them receded in broader society. The conflict was remembered as a "brothers' war" pitting Northern against Southern whites. Well beyond the borders of the South, memory of the Lost Cause of the Confederacy, a symbol of local self-government and individual rebelliousness, long remained a potent cultural force in American life.

Among historians, all this began to change after World War II. If World War I, with its massive slaughter and disappointing aftermath, had fueled Civil War revisionism by instilling skepticism about war in general, the Good War proved that in certain circumstances military action is necessary and desirable. In an influential article in 1949, historian Arthur Schlesinger Jr. challenged the underlying premise of prevailing Civil War scholarship. The South, he pointed out, had shown no evidence of a willingness to end slavery; indeed, over time it had become ever more hysterical in its defense. With one eye firmly on the recent past, Schlesinger insisted that a society closed in support of evil could not be appeased, and if it was worth a war to destroy Nazism, surely it was worth one to eradicate slavery. But not until the 1960s, under the impact of the civil rights revolution, did historians en masse repudiate a half-century of Civil War scholarship, concluding that the war resulted from an irreconcilable conflict between two fundamentally different societies, one resting

on slavery, the other on free labor. Historians pushed emancipation to the center of their account of the Civil War, and it has
remained there ever since.

* * *

If historians have reached a considerable degree of consensus, the
same cannot be said of the general public. Americans do not share
either a single understanding of the war's meaning or a unified
conception of its relevance to our own times. Nor, as the war's
sesquicentennial progresses, do we appear to be in a celebratory
mood. In the wake of Iraq, a truly needless war cynically justified
in the language of freedom, many Americans seem reluctant to
commemorate an earlier conflict. A number of recent books have
insisted that the Civil War—and indeed all war—has no meaning other than death and destruction, and that by ascribing lofty
motives to the combatants, historians fall into the trap of legiti-
mizing past and present carnage.

Both left and right have grown more suspicious of exercises of
power by the national state. Civil libertarians are appalled by the
persistent violations of individual freedoms since September 11.
The party of Lincoln, its center of gravity now located in the states
of the old Confederacy, has little desire to recall a time when its
ancestors believed in a federal government that actively promoted
racial equality and paid for war with tariffs and taxes (including
the dreaded income tax, inaugurated in 1862). Nostalgia for the
Confederacy survives in Tea Party and broader right-wing circles.
Moreover, the whole business of historical commemoration has
been somewhat tarnished of late. Ever since 1992, when Native

Americans and their allies disrupted efforts to celebrate the 500th anniversary of Columbus's first voyage by drawing attention to the deleterious consequences that flowed from the European conquest of the Western Hemisphere, historical anniversaries have exposed fault lines in today's society.

As always, a gap remains between historical scholarship and popular understandings of history. Fifty years ago, when Charleston, South Carolina, marked the anniversary of the firing on Fort Sumter, the city was bedecked with Confederate flags and the commemorations made no mention of slavery. This past April, the city fathers and National Park Service sponsored a gathering that included reflections on slavery's role in the war and on post-slavery race relations. As in 1961, a band played "Dixie," but this time "The Battle Hymn of the Republic" accompanied it, recognition that a majority of South Carolina's population (the slaves) sided with the Union, not the Confederacy. But the event attracted far smaller crowds than fifty years ago.

Of course, the centennial celebrations of the 1960s took place at the high tide of the civil rights revolution, which underscored the Civil War's continuing relevance. A century after the war began, passions over the war did not seem to have diminished; at a gathering in April 1961 to mark the anniversary of the firing on Fort Sumter, the Headquarters Hotel in Charleston denied accommodations to a black delegate from New Jersey. In response, President Kennedy moved the event to a nearby naval base, whereupon Southern delegates seceded to hold their own Confederate States Centennial Conference.

A half-century later, the election of the nation's first black president has produced the ironic result of largely removing issues related to the legacy of Emancipation from the national agenda. In the absence of a vibrant movement for racial justice and in an era that has been labeled "postracial," the relevance of the Civil War appears far less clear than it did fifty years ago. In 1963 it seemed entirely appropriate for Martin Luther King Jr. to begin his "I Have a Dream" speech at the Lincoln Memorial with a reference to the unfulfilled promise of the Emancipation Proclamation. Such rhetoric is rarely heard today, when the black freedom struggle, intensely divisive when it took place, has been transformed into a narrative of national unity, a fulfillment of bedrock American principles rather than the "revolution in values" called for by King. Even neo-Confederates portray the Old South as a multicultural paradise of racial harmony and invent imaginary legions of black Confederate soldiers to demonstrate that both sides can claim credit for the end of slavery.

In a society in which everyone from Glenn Beck to President Obama assumes the mantle of the civil rights movement, slavery seems not to arouse as much interest as in the past. Polls show that a majority of Americans identify issues other than slavery—states' rights, the tariff, etc.—as the war's fundamental cause. Yet contemporaries had little doubt that slavery "somehow" lay at the root of the conflict, as Lincoln put it in his Second Inaugural Address, and that emancipation was its most profound outcome. The Confederacy's founders forthrightly announced that they had created a republic whose "cornerstone," as Confederate Vice President

Alexander Stephens declared, was the principle that "slavery, subordination to the superior race," was the "natural and moral condition" of black Americans. When Bismarck identified preservation of the Union as the war's purpose, Grant corrected him: "Not only to save the Union, but destroy slavery … a stain to the Union." Despite America's post-Reconstruction retreat from the ideal of equality, the destruction of slavery remains an epochal victory for human rights, worthy of celebration. Moreover, as Lincoln recognized, the service of black soldiers, most of them emancipated slaves, proved essential to Union victory. No narrative of the Civil War can ignore the centrality of slavery to its origins, conduct and legacy.

This past May at a ceremony in Paris, French President Nicolas Sarkozy unveiled a monument to the victims of slavery (something we have yet to erect in the United States). Its inscription reads: "By their struggles and their strong desire for dignity and liberty, the slaves of the French colonies contributed to the universality of human rights and to the ideal of liberty, equality and fraternity that is the foundation of our republic." In other words, the monument posits not simply that the nation conferred freedom on the slaves but that it learned about freedom, in part, from them. Here is a model of sober celebration, of triumph laced with humility, that we might seek to emulate. ❖

Warped History

Dylann Roof, the accused murderer of nine men and women in the Emanuel AME Church in Charleston, South Carolina, is clearly a disturbed individual. Yet the language he drew on to justify his crime demonstrates the enduring power of historical myths and memories. Before opening fire on his victims, Roof reportedly explained his actions by saying, "You are raping our women and taking over the country." This supposed need to save white women from black rapists has deep historical roots. It was invoked to legitimate the violent overthrow of Reconstruction, the nation's first experiment in interracial democracy. Black victims of lynching in South Carolina and elsewhere were often described as rapists, even though, as the anti-lynching crusader Ida B. Wells pointed out, in nearly every case the accusation was a "bare lie." A black rapist was a pivotal figure in *The Birth of a Nation*, the 1915 film that glorified the Ku Klux Klan. Claude Bowers's influential 1929 history of the post–Civil War years, *The Tragic Era*, described rape in the South as the product of the political rights blacks achieved during

Reconstruction—a ludicrous statement in view of the countless black women who suffered sexual assault under slavery. Roof's complaint that blacks were "taking over" the state echoes justifications for racist violence during and after Reconstruction and the disenfranchisement of black voters in the 1890s.

Roof has a sense of history, warped though it may be. He claims to have read "hundreds" of slave narratives, all demonstrating, to his satisfaction, how benevolently slaves were treated—an idea long discredited by historians, but still encountered on white-supremacist websites and conservative talk-radio shows. He had himself photographed not only with the flags of the Confederacy, apartheid South Africa, and Rhodesia, during its short-lived period of independence under white domination, but at a slave plantation. He knows enough to have chosen the Emanuel Church, long a vital center of black life and politics, to strike his blow against the black community.

Emanuel was the place of worship not only of Denmark Vesey, who plotted a slave insurrection in Charleston in 1822, but also of the Rev. Richard H. Cain, who occupied Emanuel's pulpit during Reconstruction. Like his successor, the murder victim Clementa Pinckney, Cain used the church as a springboard to public service, including a term in the state Senate, where he worked to provide former slaves with access to land. Later, as a member of Congress, Cain rebuked a white Representative who referred to slavery as a civilizing institution for black "barbarians" (not unlike Roof's outlook). His colleague's concept of civilization, Cain replied, seemed to amount to little more than "the lash and whipping post." Unlike Pinckney, Cain did not fall victim to violence, but he and his family lived "in constant fear" and his home was guarded day and night by armed men.

I have taught in South Carolina and lectured in the state numerous times. I have unfailingly been treated with courtesy and respect. Roof does not speak for all the white people in the state. Nonetheless, South Carolina has never really come to terms with its tortured history. Here are a few highlights of the state's extreme pro-slavery, white-supremacist past. In 1776, South Carolina delegates to the Continental Congress forced Thomas Jefferson to remove a clause condemning slavery from the Declaration of Independence. In 1787, South Carolinians were primarily responsible for the Constitution's fugitive slave clause and provision allowing the importation of slaves from abroad to continue for twenty additional years. Until 1860, a tight-knit coterie of plantation owners controlled the state; they did not even allow the white citizens to vote in presidential elections (the legislature chose the state's members of the electoral college).

Before the Civil War, South Carolina was one of two states, along with Mississippi, where nearly a majority of white families owned slaves, and had the largest black majority in its population (nearly 60 percent in 1860). This combination produced a unique brand of extremism in defense of slavery. The state was the birthplace of nullification, the first to secede, and the site of the first shot of the Civil War. During Reconstruction, black Carolinians enjoyed a brief moment of civil equality and genuine political power, but this ended with a violent "Redemption," followed by decades of Jim Crow. More recently, South Carolina led the Southern walkout from the 1948 Democratic National Convention to protest a civil rights plank in the party's platform, and supported its native son, Strom Thurmond, who ran as the "Dixiecrat" candidate for president. In 1964, it was one of five states of the Deep South to vote for Barry Goldwater, paving the way for the Republicans' "Southern strategy" of appealing to white resentment against black civil rights gains.

Nor is the Charleston massacre the only instance of mass murder of South Carolinian blacks. During Reconstruction the Ku Klux Klan launched a reign of terror in parts of the state that led to dozens of deaths. The Hamburg Massacre of 1876, where several blacks were murdered in cold blood, was a crucial step in the overthrow of Reconstruction. At Orangeburg in 1968, officers of the state highway patrol killed three black college students and wounded more than twenty others. Unfortunately, this incident has been largely forgotten, unlike the killings of white students two years later at Kent State.

Ideas about history legitimate and shape the present, and public presentations of history tell us a great deal about a society's values. As in other Southern states, statues of Confederate generals, Klansmen and segregationists dot the South Carolina landscape. Although a statue was erected recently in Charleston to Denmark Vesey, and historic sites like Drayton Hall plantation and the National Park Service's Fort Sumter site have revised their presentations to deal directly with the black experience, South Carolina has no monument to the victims of slavery and hardly any to black leaders of Reconstruction or other eras. It took until 1998 for a portrait of Jonathan J. Wright, who served during Reconstruction as the first African-American justice of the South Carolina Supreme Court, to join the paintings of all the state's white justices in the court building.

This warped public display of history confronts South Carolinians, white and black, every day with a stark message about who rules the state. South Carolina's leaders cannot abolish the hate that spews forth on the Internet. But if they are serious about changing the way the state remembers and represents its history, let them erect not only a memorial to Reverend Pinckney and the other victims but also statues of the black leaders of Reconstruction and of courageous figures of the civil rights era such as Levi Pearson, who in 1947 filed suit against his child's school district to protest the inadequate funding of black education and saw his home attacked in retaliation.

The burgeoning movement to take down the Confederate flag in South Carolina and other states is an important first step. Even after it is gone, however, the public display of history in South Carolina will remain biased and one-dimensional. That, among many other things, needs to change. ✤

An American Birthright

SEPTEMBER 14, 2015

Birthright citizenship—the principle that any person born in the United States is automatically a citizen— has been embedded in the Constitution since the ratification of the 14th Amendment in 1868. This summer, it has suddenly emerged as a major issue in the Republican presidential campaign. Following the lead of Donald Trump, candidates like Rick Santorum, Bobby Jindal, Ted Cruz and Rand Paul have called for the repeal or reinterpretation of the amendment, to prevent children born to undocumented immigrants from being recognized as American citizens.

The situation abounds in ironies. Now a Republican target, the 14th Amendment was for many decades considered a crowning achievement of what once called itself the party of Lincoln. Today, moreover, birthright citizenship stands as an example of the much-abused idea of American exceptionalism, which Republicans have berated President Obama for supposedly not embracing. Many things claimed as uniquely American—a devotion to individual freedom, for example, or social opportunity—exist in other countries. But birthright citizenship does make the United States (along with Canada) unique in the developed world. No European nation recognizes the principle. Yet, oddly, those most insistent on proclaiming their belief in American exceptionalism seem keenest on abolishing it.

Why is birthright citizenship part of our Constitution? Until after the Civil War, there existed no commonly agreed-upon definition of American citizenship or the rights that it entailed. The original Constitution mentioned citizens but did not delineate who they were. The individual states determined the boundaries and rights of citizenship.

The Constitution does, however, empower Congress to create a system of naturalization, and a law of 1790 offered the first legislative definition of American nationality. Although the new nation proclaimed itself, in the words of Thomas Paine, an "asylum for mankind," that law restricted the process of becoming a citizen from abroad to any "free white person." Thus, at the outset, ideas of American citizenship were closely linked to race.

Slaves, of course, were not part of the body politic. But in 1860, there were half a million free blacks in the United States, nearly all of them born in this country. For decades, their citizenship had been hotly contested. Finally, in the *Dred Scott* decision of 1857, the Supreme Court declared that no black person could be a citizen. The framers of the Constitution, Chief Justice Roger Taney insisted, regarded blacks, free and slave, as "beings of an inferior order, and altogether unfit to associate with the white race ... and so far inferior, that they had no rights which the white man was bound to respect." (This statement, the Radical Republican leader Thaddeus Stevens later remarked, "damned [Taney] to everlasting fame; and, I fear, to everlasting fire.")

The destruction of slavery in the Civil War, coupled with the service of 200,000 black men in the Union army and navy, put the question of black citizenship on the national agenda. The era of Reconstruction produced the first formal delineation of American citizenship, a vast expansion of citizens' rights, and a repudiation of the idea that these rights attached to persons in their capacity as members of certain ethnic or racial groups, rather than as part of an undifferentiated American people. Birthright citizenship is one expression of the commitment to equality and the expansion of national consciousness that marked Reconstruction.

In June 1866, Congress approved and sent to the states the 14th Amendment, whose opening section declares that "all persons born or naturalized in the United States, and subject to the jurisdiction thereof, are citizens of the United States and of the state wherein they reside." What persons are not subject to national jurisdiction? The debates in Congress in 1866 make clear that the language was meant to exclude Native Americans, still considered members of their tribal sovereignties. Two minuscule other groups were mentioned: children born in the United States to the wives of foreign diplomats, and those fathered by members of occupying armies (fortunately, the latter case hasn't arisen since the amendment's ratification).

While the immediate purpose of this part of the 14th Amendment was to invalidate the *Dred Scott* decision, the language says nothing about race—it was meant to establish a principle applicable to all. Opponents raised the specter of Chinese citizenship, or citizenship for "gypsies"; one senator said that he'd heard more about gypsies during the debate than in his entire previous life. Lyman Trumbull, chairman of the Senate Judiciary Committee, made it crystal clear that "all persons" meant what it said: Children born to Chinese, gypsies, or anybody else one could think of would be citizens.

What about the children of "illegal aliens" today? No such group existed in 1866; at the time, just about anyone who wished to enter the United States was free to do so. Only later did the law single out certain groups for exclusion: prostitutes, polygamists, lunatics, anarchists and, starting in 1882, the entire population of China. In fact, the closest analogy to today's debate concerns children born to the 50,000 or so Chinese in the United States in 1866, all of whose parents were ineligible for citizenship. The authors of the amendment, and subsequent decisions by the Supreme Court, made it clear that these children must be considered American citizens. The legal status of the parents does not determine the rights of the child; anyone born here can be a good American. These are the principles the Republicans now seek to overturn.

The 14th Amendment, as Republican editor George Curtis wrote, was part of a process that changed the US government from one "for white men" to one "for mankind." Birthright citizenship is one legacy of the titanic struggle of the Reconstruction era to create a genuine democracy grounded in the principle of equality. It remains an eloquent statement of what our country is or would like to be. We should think long and hard before abandoning it. ❖

Letter to Bernie

NOVEMBER 16, 2015

Dear Senator Sanders,

Congratulations on the tremendous success of your campaign. You have energized and inspired millions of Americans and forced the questions of economic inequality and excessive corporate power to the center of our political discourse. These are remarkable accomplishments.

So take the following advice as coming from an admirer. I urge you to reconsider how you respond to the inevitable questions about what you mean by democratic socialism and peaceful revolution. The next time, embrace our own American radical tradition. There's nothing wrong with Denmark; we can learn a few things from them (and vice-versa). But most Americans don't know or care much about Scandinavia. More important, your response inadvertently reinforces the idea that socialism is a foreign import. Instead, talk about our radical forebears here in the United States, for the most successful radicals have always spoken the language of American society and appealed to some of its deepest values.

You could begin with Tom Paine and other American revolutionaries who strove not simply for independence from Britain but to free the new nation from the social and economic inequalities of Europe. Embrace the tradition of abolitionists, black and white, men and women like William Lloyd Garrison, Frederick Douglass and Abby Kelley, who, against overwhelming odds, broke through the conspiracy of silence of the two major parties on the issue of slavery and helped to create a public sentiment that led to Lincoln's election and emancipation. (And don't forget to mention that slaves represented by far the largest concentration of wealth in the United States on the eve of the Civil War, that slaveholders were the richest Americans of their time, and that nothing could be accomplished without confronting their economic and political power.) Refer to the long struggle for women's rights, which demanded not only the vote but also equality for women in all realms of life and in doing so challenged some of the most powerful entrenched interests in the country.

You should mention the People's Party, or Populists, and their Omaha platform of 1892, which describes a nation not unlike our own, with inequality rife and a political system in need of change, where "corruption dominates the ballot-box, the Legislatures, the Congress, and touches even the ermine of the bench. ... [and] the fruits of the toil of millions are boldly stolen to build up colossal fortunes for a few." Or what about the Progressive platform of 1912, for a party that nominated Theodore Roosevelt for president, which called, among other things, for strict limits on campaign contributions, universal health insurance, vigorous federal oversight of giant corporations and other measures that, over a century later, have yet to be realized.

Of course, every politician gives lip service to the idea of enhancing economic opportunity, but you have, rightly, emphasized that to secure this requires the active involvement of the federal government, not simply letting the free market work its supposed magic. Your antecedents include not just FDR's New Deal but also his Second Bill of Rights of 1944, inspired by the era's labor movement, which called for the government to guarantee to all Americans the rights to employment, education, medical care, a decent home and other entitlements that are out of reach for too many today. You could point to A. Philip Randolph's Freedom Budget of 1967, which asked the government to address the deep economic inequalities the civil rights revolution had left untouched. But beyond these and other examples, the point is that the rights we enjoy today—civil, political, economic, social—are the result of struggles of the past, not gifts from on high. That's what you mean when you say we need a citizens' revolution.

As to socialism, the term today refers not to a blueprint for a future society but to the need to rein in the excesses of capitalism, evident all around us, to empower ordinary people in a political system verging on plutocracy, and to develop policies that make opportunity real for the millions of Americans for whom it is not. This is what it meant in the days of Eugene V. Debs, the great labor leader and Socialist candidate for president who won almost a million votes in 1912. Debs spoke the language of what he called "political equality and economic freedom." But equally important, as Debs emphasized, socialism is as much a moral idea as an economic one—the conviction that vast inequalities of wealth, power and opportunity are simply wrong and that ordinary people, using political power, can produce far-reaching change. It was Debs's moral fervor as much as his specific program that made him beloved by millions of Americans.

Each generation of Americans has made its own contribution to an ongoing radical tradition, and you are following in their footsteps. So next time, forget about Denmark and talk about Paine, Douglass, FDR and Debs as forebears of a movement that can make the United States a fairer, more equal, more just society. ✤

Sincerely,
Eric Foner

Teaching the
History of American
Radicalism in the Age of Obama

Last spring, I taught my final class at Columbia University, and now I'm riding off into the sunset of retirement. The course, which attracted some 180 students, was called "The Radical Tradition in America." Beginning with the American Revolution, it explored the ideas, tactics, strengths, weaknesses, and interconnections of the movements that have attempted to change American society—from abolitionism and feminism to the labor movement, socialism, communism, black radicalism, the New Left, Occupy Wall Street, and Black Lives Matter. Although the word "radicalism" is often applied to those on the right as well as the left, I announced at the outset that, since we had only one semester, I planned to focus on what might be called left-wing radicalism. Those students who wanted exposure to right-wing radicalism, I added, could enroll in any class in Columbia's business school.

Teaching the class as Barack Obama's presidency neared its end and Senator Bernie Sanders's campaign ignited the enthusiasm of millennials was an interesting experience. I began with the premise that radicalism has been a persistent feature of our history and that radicals, while often castigated as foreign-inspired enemies of American institutions, have usually sprung from our culture, spoken its language, and appealed to some of our deepest values—facts that help to explain radicalism's persistence even in the face of tenacious opposition. American radicalism entails a visionary aspiration to remake the world on the basis of greater equality—economic, legal, social, racial, or sexual. Despite the occasional resort to violence, most of these movements have reflected the democratic ethos of American life: they've been open rather than secretive and have relied on education, example, or political action rather than coercion. Not surprisingly, they have also reflected some of the larger society's flaws; radicals are a product of their society, no matter how fully they reject certain aspects of it. While I made clear my sympathy with most of the groups we studied, I also insisted that we should not be surprised that some abolitionists were antifeminist, some feminists racist, some labor organizations hostile to immigrants. Neither history nor politics is well served by simple hagiography.

From Thomas Paine's ideal of an America freed from the hereditary inequalities of Europe, to the vision of liberation from legal and customary bondage espoused by abolitionists and feminists; from the Knights of Labor's concept of a cooperative commonwealth, to the socialists' call for workers to organize society in accordance with their own aspirations; from the New Left's embrace of personal liberation as a goal every bit as worthy as material abundance, to the current efforts to counteract the less appealing consequences of globalization, each generation has made its distinctive contribution to an ongoing radical tradition. Many achievements that we think of as the most admirable in our history are to a considerable extent the outgrowth of American radicalism, including the abolition of slavery, the dramatic expansion of women's rights, the respect for civil liberties and our right of dissent, and the efforts today to tame a rampant capitalism and combat economic inequality. Many of our current ideas about freedom, equality, and the rights of citizens originated with American radicals.

More than any other movement, I told my students, abolitionism provided the template for how to achieve radical change in America. The abolitionists' first task was to destroy the conspiracy of silence by which political parties, churches, and other institutions sought to exclude slavery from public debate. While differing among themselves on strategy and tactics, abolitionists understood that radical change requires the cooperation of an engaged social movement and enlightened political leadership. Long after the Civil War, organized labor, Populists, advocates of women's rights, and many other radical activists looked to the crusade against slavery as an inspiration and a model, and in slogans like "wage slavery" and "the slavery of sex" adapted its language to their own concerns. I also devoted a good deal of time to the long struggle for women's equality and how it challenged fundamental aspects of American society, including the idea of "separate spheres" for men and women; the doctrine of coverture, whereby a married women's legal identity was subsumed into her husband's; and the demarcation of the family as a site insulated from questions of power, rights, and oppression.

Obama's 2008 campaign, which mobilized millions of people new to politics, served as an illustration of the symbiotic relationship between popular movements and political action. Unfortunately, even before Obama assumed office, it became clear that he had little interest in building upon the popular upsurge that helped to elect him. A revealing moment came at a press conference at the end of November 2008, when he was asked how he reconciled his campaign slogan, "Change We Can Believe In," with the appointment of an economic team largely composed of the same neoliberal ideologues who had helped bring about the financial crisis. "The vision for change," Obama replied, "comes … first and foremost … from me." As I mentioned to my class, one can compare Obama's top-down remark to a comment attributed to the early twentieth-century socialist Eugene Debs: "I would not lead you to the promised land if I could, because if I could lead you in, someone else could lead you out." Debs understood that movements, not just political leaders, make social change possible. Obama has never really learned that lesson. To be sure, he sought to cultivate an identification with history by embracing the civil rights movement, though this is hardly a controversial stance at a time when Martin Luther King Jr.'s birthday is a national holiday and even Glenn Beck claims his legacy. But even then, Obama embraced a sanitized version in which the movement represents a fulfillment of basic American ideals, not the unfulfilled "revolution of values" that King hoped to see. Obama doesn't invoke the radical King who spoke of "democratic socialism," launched the Poor People's Campaign, and supported the antiwar movement.

Another historical figure that Obama has consciously channeled is Abraham Lincoln. He announced his candidacy in 2007 in Springfield, Illinois, Lincoln's hometown, and took the oath of office on the same Bible that Lincoln used for his inauguration. But unlike Lincoln, who respected people to his left such as the abolitionist Frederick Douglass and the Radical Republican leader Charles Sumner and took their objections to some of his policies seriously, Obama seems to view criticism as little more than an annoyance. He has accused liberal critics of being sanctimonious purists, more interested in staking out a principled position than in getting things done. Lincoln welcomed criticism; Obama, who has always considered himself (and often has been) "the smartest guy in the room," doesn't appear to think that he has much to learn from others. Alternative viewpoints never seemed to penetrate his administration's inner sanctum.

"The American Radical Tradition" was never a simple course to teach. It presumed a basic knowledge of "mainstream" American history that not every undergraduate has, and it attracted an unusually diverse group of students, from history majors looking to complete departmental requirements to activists in search of a usable past. Many students, nonetheless, seemed to enjoy learning a history that few had encountered before. The online evaluations asked students to record what they took away from the course. "This class gave me a totally new perspective on American history," said one. "The course taught me how to approach American history with a critical lens," said another. And a third, perhaps a bit overenthusiastically, proclaimed: "I learned how to start a revolution."

I taught a version of this course every three to four years since the mid-1970s. Given the conservative climate that has gripped our politics and the marginalization felt by many activist students, I've usually concluded it by warning against discouragement and reminding the class that every generation of Americans has witnessed some kind of radical upsurge. Despite overwhelming odds, I pointed out, Douglass, Debs, King, Elizabeth Cady Stanton, Margaret Sanger, Malcolm X, and the many others we studied did not give up hope: they were willing to fight and lose for a long time before achieving even partial success. It's important to remember that all revolutions are unfinished, all triumphs incomplete, and every success or failure simply sets up the next series of struggles.

This past spring, those warnings proved unnecessary. I was afraid that disappointment with Washington gridlock and the modest parameters of change during the Obama years would have left my students disillusioned with politics. I needn't have worried: whatever their thoughts about Obama, so many of them were energized by the Sanders insurgency that 2016 turned out to be a propitious moment for teaching the history of radicalism. Like many upsurges of radicalism in the past, Bernie's came as a complete surprise. Not long ago, the historian Steve Fraser published *The Age of Acquiescence*, which compared the first Gilded Age with our own and grimly concluded that, unlike in the late nineteenth century, popular resistance doesn't exist today. Fraser recently acknowledged that he'll have to rethink that conclusion, because one of the achievements of the Sanders campaign was to crack open the lingering constraints of Cold War ideology and make economic inequality a part of the public discourse. More than a century ago, the German sociologist Werner Sombart famously asked, "Why is there no socialism in America?" The question these days is rather: "Why did so many voters support a self-proclaimed democratic socialist for president?" One poll found that among people ages 18 to 24, a higher percentage had a favorable opinion of socialism than of capitalism—a result that shouldn't be surprising in view of the acute dysfunctionality of existing capitalism.

Whether the enthusiasm generated by the Sanders campaign will survive the recent election is difficult to say, but it requires a historical perspective to understand its roots and possibilities. Although in some ways a complete surprise, Sanders's challenge did not spring from the void: its emergence was foretold by the Seattle demonstrations against the World Trade Organization in 1999 and, more recently, by Occupy Wall Street and similar protests around the country; the movement for a $15 minimum wage; the remarkable success of Thomas Piketty's *Capital in the Twenty-First Century*; and the movements against the deportation of immigrants, mass incarceration, and police mistreatment of people of color. As it unfolded, Bernie's campaign offered me numerous opportunities to link the past and the present. The day the *New York Times* endorsed Hillary Clinton for the Democratic nomination on the grounds that Sanders wasn't pragmatic enough, my students discussed the antislavery movement. "What exactly constitutes political practicality?" I asked them. For much of the 1850s and the first two years of the Civil War, Lincoln—widely considered the model of a pragmatic politician—advocated a plan to end slavery that involved gradual emancipation, monetary compensation for slave owners, and setting up colonies of freed blacks outside the United States. This harebrained scheme had no possibility of enactment. It was the abolitionists, still viewed by some historians as irresponsible fanatics, who put forward the program—an immediate and uncompensated end to slavery, with black people becoming US citizens—that came to pass (with Lincoln's eventual help, of course).

Each time I taught "The American Radical Tradition," I concluded by predicting (with greater confidence at some times than others) the emergence of a new generation of American radicals. I reminded my students that radicalism has always been hard work. There is truth in Oscar Wilde's witticism, "The problem with socialism is that it takes up too many evenings." But today, we live in a moment of opportunity. As Antonio Gramsci observed at the end of World War I, the old order is dying, but the new one cannot yet be born. For a while after the end of the Cold War, it seemed like we were condemned to live in a world where the only alternatives to unregulated capitalism were religious fundamentalism or xenophobia and racism. Then the financial collapse of 2008 drove a stake through the heart of neoliberalism, the dominant ideology of the past generation (although its ghost still walks the earth, including the corridors of the Obama administration). The great achievement of the Sanders campaign was to step into the vacuum and begin to offer a new vision. The election of Donald Trump, while disastrous in so many ways, is yet another illustration of the bankruptcy of neoliberalism and offers the Left an opportunity to forge a new set of policies to promote political, social, and economic equality.

Any new radicalism needs to learn from the past, but not simply to reenact it. The new American radicalism must be open and multifaceted, speaking the language of American society but receptive to insights from an increasingly interconnected world. One thing I think we've learned is that pinning one's hopes on a single individual (including Obama and Sanders) is a recipe for disappointment. Maintaining the energy of popular mobilizations takes precedence over devotion to any individual. Nor is there a need for a single "party line": abolitionists and feminists both divided into a host of small groups. Following different, even contradictory paths—voting or nonvoting, industrial or craft unionism, integration or black nationalism—may well produce greater strength, rather than fragmentation and weakness. At the same time, single-focus organizations, which have proliferated in the last generation, need to recapture the sense of being part of a larger movement for social change that addresses diverse groups and interests—something that the

Socialist Party before World War I went at least part of the way toward embodying.

On the first page of the course syllabus, I always included the words of Max Weber, a rebuke to those who believe that critics of society should set their sights only on "practical" measures: "What is possible would never have been achieved if, in this world, people had not repeatedly reached for the impossible." ♣

A Usable Past: An Interview

On July 20, 2016, the day after the Republican National Convention officially nominated Donald J. Trump as the presidential candidate of the party whose origins Eric Foner chronicled in his first book, Free Soil, Free Labor, Free Men *(1969), I met with Foner in his office at Columbia University. The following transcript of our conversation has been lightly edited and condensed.*

—Richard Kreitner, Assistant Editor, *The Nation*

Richard Kreitner: How did you come to be acquainted with *The Nation*?

Eric Foner: I grew up in a left-wing household, so *The Nation* and *I.F. Stone's Weekly* came to our house periodically. I can't say I was particularly well informed as a kid, but later I began reading it more seriously when I was an undergraduate student, as all the events of the 1960s were taking place. It was on my radar screen, but I can't say I had any particular connection to it, until 1977, when the magazine's publisher, James Storrow, called me out of the blue and asked for something on the fiftieth anniversary of the Sacco-Vanzetti case. I thought it was an interesting idea, even though most of my work up to that point was about nineteenth-century history, except for the book on Tom Paine I'd just published. That's probably what made him think I knew about radicals. So I did a lot of research for it, and that article connected me with *The Nation*.

Once Victor Navasky became editor shortly after that, he really got me interested in becoming more involved in *The Nation*, and then at some point, I can't remember quite when, I was invited to join the editorial board...

R.K.: I believe it was 1996.

E.F.: It was that long ago? Well, most of my writing has been since then, not all of it though. Obviously *The Nation* has a very important history, it has a very important role within American history, it has a very important role today in American politics, and I'm very happy to be associated with it.

R.K.: Was that Sacco-Vanzetti piece your first foray into a journalistic forum, or had you written for other places?

E.F.: I'd written some pieces for the *New York Times Book Review*. I wrote for a thing called *University Review*, which was sort of a left-wing publication of the late 1960s, early '70s. You know, my PhD supervisor was Richard Hofstadter, and even though his politics were not identical with mine, he always emphasized writing for a general public. Write good, academic, scholarly history, he said, but write in a way that can reach a broader audience. He did it brilliantly. That was just part of our education here at Columbia, trying to figure out ways to reach an audience outside the ivory tower.

R.K.: Was that a more uncommon sentiment then than it is today?

E.F.: I think it was uncommon, though perhaps not in New York, which had the "New York Intellectuals," who made a point of reaching a wider audience. But that was confined to a very specific world. They were New Yorkers. They were Jewish. They were writing about Cold War issues, more or less. The 1960s produced a new generation who were beginning to write in other places—this wasn't exactly a mass-market publication, but I was involved in founding a short-lived journal called *Marxist Perspectives* in the 1970s, which was academic but aimed at trying to encourage Marxist dialogue about historical, political, sociological and other issues. The idea of moving outside purely the scholarly venue was certainly in the air at that time.

R.K.: One of the early pieces in the book is the review with Jon Wiener about the Smithsonian's exhibit on American art and the West. It's both a response and a contribution to the culture wars. A lot of people say those battles are over and we won.

E.F.: Well, they should look at the Republican National Convention if they think the culture wars are over! By the time that piece was published, I had somehow serendipitously developed a part-time vocation in museum exhibitions. In the late 1980s I was invited to be the co-curator of a big exhibit on Lincoln and the Civil War at the Chicago Historical Society. After that I worked on an exhibit about the Reconstruction period. I was into the question of museums and how they can present a more up-to-date history. And then, to the surprise of historians, history became a ground for the culture wars, largely through the efforts of Lynne Cheney to torpedo the National History Standards in 1994. But that argument became, "Why are historians tearing down our national ideology? Why are they trying to say bad things about our great leaders of the past? Why are they emphasizing slavery and the fate of Native Americans—all these depressing things? We have to gird ourselves for the great struggles ahead. We need history to promote patriotism among our young people." One of the high or low points of my career was debating, in 1995 or so, Lynne Cheney on Pat Buchanan's TV show, *Crossfire*. That was a lively occasion, with us yelling at each other the whole time.

I wanted to be engaged in those issues. So Jon and I—Jon is an old, old friend—we went to the Smithsonian and looked at the exhibit. There had been a lot of debate about it, and we thought this was an important issue—public history, the presentation of history outside the academy. Those wars are not over. They're still debating whether the Confederate flag can be flown, what to do with monuments in the South, what to do with the names of slave owners and other racists on public buildings, and so on. I wish it were true that the culture war was over and the left had won. There's certainly a wider acceptance today of a more sophisticated, complicated view of American history than people like Lynne Cheney wanted to promote back then. The country is much more diversified, and people are aware of that in a way, and that has helped to diversify our history, but these debates are continuing.

R.K.: Since you mentioned it, what is your position on the battles over monuments, school names, emblems and so on?

E.F.: My position is that it depends, which is not a very clear answer. This is a very important debate. Every situation has its own context. Should we take down the statue of Thomas Jefferson here at Columbia because he was a major slave owner? It's in front of the journalism building. Jefferson was a big advocate of freedom of the press, freedom of speech—it's appropriate. Should Yale have a college named after John C. Calhoun? I don't think so. I'm not a Yale person, so in a sense it's not my business. But I wouldn't want to be in that college. Calhoun was *the* major pro-slavery ideologue of the first half of the nineteenth century. To my mind this would be like having a college named after Goebbels or anyone who was a propagandist for Nazi Germany. My general feeling is that we should add *more* monuments, rather than take them away. I don't have an objection to a monument of a Confederate soldier in the South. That's part of their history. But how come there are no monuments to black leaders of Reconstruction—the governors, the senators, the members of Congress, the local leaders? There are literally two, I think. The problem is not that you have monuments to slave owners but that the public history is completely one-sided. It makes it seem like that is the sole history of the South when there are other parts of the history, and not just African-American, that also deserve to be represented in the public displays of historical memory. I don't think the Confederate flag should be flown at the statehouse in South Carolina. That's a public venue that's supposed to represent all South Carolinians. Put it in the museum, or something like that. But these are healthy debates about what our history is and how we should present it to the public. I'm very happy those debates are taking place.

R.K.: I was just reading your introduction to *Tom Paine and Revolutionary America*, where you said that your aim in writing about the history of American radicalism was, in part, "to provide modern-day social activists with a 'usable past.'" What does the phrase mean to you?

E.F.: The "usable past" is a term that became popular in the late 1960s. Howard Zinn used it; Jesse Lemisch used it. Radical historians began talking about it. I like the term because the past should be usable. That does not mean propaganda. A distorted past is not useful. A past like the one I was taught in school when I was growing up is not a usable past. It was just about how America was created perfect and has just been getting better ever since.

R.K.: That seems usable for the Cheneys.

E.F.: But it wasn't, really, because when the 1960s came along, it was impossible to figure out how the past that we had learned about had produced this. Since all our problems had been solved, what were people complaining about? It was a past without black people, without Native Americans. A much better past was created—a truer, more accurate, more honest past was created by several generations of historians. For those who want social change, knowing how social change took place in the past is a very valuable thing. That doesn't mean you just create a Hall of Fame of great leaders of the past—that guy was great, this woman was great. That's not what I'm talking about. History does inform the present, and it should. That's what I mean by a usable past: a historical consciousness that can enable us to address the problems of society today in an intelligent manner.

R.K.: Around the inauguration of George W. Bush, it seems, your writing for *The Nation* took something of a turn, becoming more exclusively about the use and abuse of history by conservatives. What do you recall of your thinking at the time?

E.F.: Like many, many others, I was utterly appalled by the Bush administration, the 'USA PATRIOT Act', the invasion of Iraq, the mobilization of a particular view of history to try to justify the unjustifiable. It's not like previous presidents haven't been distorting history. They all try to mobilize history to justify their policies. But I thought what Bush was doing was particularly egregious, especially since I had recently published my book on the history of freedom. They were using the idea of freedom to justify limitations on freedom. I became very alarmed.

Also, how shall I put this? By that time I was a quite prominent historian. To its credit, Columbia University is a place of real academic freedom. Nobody could do anything to me. I had a tenured professorship. I could say anything I wanted. It's not like I was a public high school teacher who feared that if they criticized the war in Iraq they would have the principal on their neck, parents calling in and saying that I'm undermining America. I spoke to people in that position. Nobody was going to do that here. My feeling was that the purpose of tenure is to enable you to speak, so if you don't speak, what is the point of tenure? So many people get used to being quiet on the road to tenure that when they get it that remains their default position. I decided I was willing to use what reputation I had to bolster the ideas that I want to put out there, even though I knew it would lead to denunciations—and it did. I was listed in books about the hundred people destroying America. I was seventy-five or seventy-six, one notch behind Latrell Spreewell, the basketball player who choked his coach. Zinn and I were the only professors on the list. My friends were jealous.

At that time the post-9/11 fever was running very high, and even an article in *The Nation* led to a lot of recriminations. But if you're going to be out there in the public sphere you have to be prepared to accept it.

R.K.: Your pieces from that time talk about other moments from our history when the populace or political leaders succumbed to fear, xenophobia and so on. So how do you tell the story of an American past that Bush, and now Trump, are either a departure from or a rejection of, if there are so many precedents for their bigotry and fearmongering?

E.F.: It's very easy to say, "Oh, Trump's gone off the reservation." But actually, this is part of the American political culture, past and present. It's not just that our politics is usually the Lincoln-Douglas debates, this high-minded discussion of important issues. Even those debates weren't like that. Douglas accused Lincoln of wanting to encourage interracial marriage. Lincoln accused Douglas of some cockamamie conspiracy with President Buchanan. Our politics has seen the low road many a time. Go back to the Know-Nothings, George Wallace, Nixon, the Southern Strategy. This is an important strand of our political culture.

That's a more frightening thought than calling Trump a lunatic and an aberration. He is the logical extension of the way the Republican Party has been operating since Goldwater, really. Of course, there are others, even the Bushes, who are appalled by this, but this is how the Republican Party has gotten votes for fifty years. Trump is just tearing off the mask. Now he just says right out the racism that was only barely hidden for so long.

We need a history that includes the nativists, the racists—an accurate history would show that it's always been there. We shouldn't just talk about how weird Trump is.

R.K.: You wrote in 2010 that it's difficult to write about Obama's presidency without a feeling of "deep disappointment." Does that feeling remain?

E.F.: My critique of Obama has not changed. Obama came into office at a very important historical moment. There was tremendous public support for him when he came in. He had a big mobilization of popular support behind him. The country was in a serious crisis. Maybe not as serious as when FDR came in, but it was really serious. You know, look what happened with FDR. He said, "We're taking action, folks!" What did Obama do? He put the same guys back in that caused the problem in the first place.

He passed a piddling little stimulus plan. He spent his whole first year fighting about healthcare and ended up with a plan that's better than nothing, but considering what was possible with sixty votes in the Senate and a majority in the House...

My disappointment is that Obama didn't seize the opportunity that was there. Now, maybe that's just Obama. He's a mainstream Democrat. We got the change that he wanted, which was minimal. But he campaigned on the promise of change with a capital C, with the backing of large numbers of people—whom he then demobilized. In November of 2008 he gave a press conference, and somebody pointed out that he was putting all the same guys back in office, and they asked where was the change. And he said something like, "I am the change." Compare that with Eugene V. Debs, who said he wouldn't lead his followers into the Promised Land even if he could, because if he could lead them in, someone else could lead them out.

So, yes, I am disappointed with Obama. It's not specific policies so much as his general approach to office, which I find too limited, given the circumstances in which he came in. After 2010, when the Republicans came into Congress, then his options became limited. But in the first two years he had a real opportunity, which he did not seize.

R.K.: So much of your work, in the magazine and in your books, has been about the politics of race in America. Does that story require some kind of retelling after the Obama years, now that we are post-postracial?

E.F.: I don't think it does. Unfortunately, the history reared up and showed itself. Those who thought that the election of Obama was the end of race in America have been sorely disappointed. I think symbolically the election of Obama was important, and will be considered important whatever future historians think of Obama. His election was a rebuke to the long history of racism in America—there's no question about that.

And yet, Obama reflects the fact that the civil rights era has created a giant gap within the black community. There is a significant stratum, of which Obama is a part, that was able to take full advantage of the opening up of opportunities, and they've moved very far up in the universities, the corporations and so on. On the other hand, there's a vast and growing class of poor blacks that has suffered enormously since the financial crisis, even under Obama. Race is now even more than ever complicated by class, and the people who are being shot by police—some of them are middle-class people but a lot of them are poor black people, and they are suffering from all sorts of things in urban areas that Obama's policies have not addressed at all. Indeed, here's the irony: the economic policies Obama pursues—free trade, bank bailouts, printing money to try to restart the economy—these are devastating for black people. Deindustrialization: that's where the solid black working class was, in factories that are disappearing. These have had serious impacts on black communities. That's not why he's pursuing them. But they're corollaries of neo-liberalism, which he supports, and it's exacerbated the problem of race in America.

R.K.: What do you think about Bernie Sanders? Is it inspiring that a self-identified socialist was able to get so far, or is it depressing that a generic FDR liberalism is seen these days as so radical?

E.F.: Well, I think he's a little more than a generic FDR liberal. I don't know what will happen with the impulse that Bernie reflected. But I think it's a major step toward what radicals try to do, what *The Nation* tries to do, which is to fill the vacuum created by the collapse of neoliberalism. The financial crisis created a political and intellectual vacuum. Neoliberalism was destroyed. Though it lingers on like a zombie walking the earth, it has no intellectual legitimacy anymore. But what is to take its place? "Democratic socialism" is a fine phrase, but it doesn't have a very worked-out substance at the moment. Nevertheless, getting people talking and thinking about alternatives is a tremendous thing, and Bernie accomplished that. What can I say? I'm fairly hopeful. But I'm always fairly hopeful, even when there's no basis for being so.

Index